THE VEGETARIAN LUNCHBASKET

225 easy, nutritious recipes for the quality-conscious family on the go

by Linda Haynes

NUCLEUS
Publications
Rte. 2 Box 49
Willow Springs, MO 65793

THE VEGETARIAN LUNCHBASKET
225 easy, nutritious recipes for the quality-conscious family on the go
by Linda Haynes

Illustrations and book design by Michael B. McClure

Published by NUCLEUS Publications, Rte. 2, Box 49, Willow Springs, MO 65793.
Send for free catalog.

First printing 1990
Second printing 1992

Library of Congress Cataloging in Publication Data
Haynes, Linda, 1951—
        The vegetarian lunchbasket / by Linda Haynes.
            p.   cm.
        ISBN 0-945934-02-5 :
        1. Vegetarian cookery. 2. Luncheons. 3. Lunchbox cookery.
    I. Title.
    TX837.H39   1990   90-6890
    641.5'636--dc20   CIP

Printed in the United States of America

For my small and large family

TABLE OF CONTENTS

Preface

The effect of food on the body is well known, and in itself encourages changing from a meat-centered diet to a vegetarian one. For example, diets high in cholesterol and fat and low in fiber, consisting primarily of meat and eggs, are linked to cancer and heart disease. Many people concerned with their health are lowering their intake of red meat and eliminating eggs. Even chicken and fish are suspect in an age of toxic chemicals and carcinogenic hormones.

The effect of food on the mind is less well researched, but interest is rising. Studies are being done with people afflicted by schizophrenia and manic-depression, with children who are hyperactive, and with various other physical and mental disorders. These show that changes in diet can have a marked impact on behavior.

Yogis (people who practice yoga, meditation and related disciplines) have known for thousands of years that food affects the mind. Certain foods help clear the mind and sharpen concentration. These are called *sentient* foods. They include vegetables, fruits, grains, nuts and seeds and dairy products. Other foods stimulate the mind so that it can be difficult to concentrate. These are called *mutative* and include foods containing caffeine and stimulating spices. A third group of foods tends to dull the mind's concentration and block it from reaching deeper levels of awareness. These foods are called *static*, and include meat, fish, poultry, eggs, onions, garlic, mushrooms, recreational drugs and alcohol.

Foods in this book are sentient, and are generally beneficial to body and mind. Recognizing that there are many ways to be a vegetarian, the author has included, where possible, alternatives to dairy products and other foods that may be restricted if you're on a low-fat or allergy diet.

It is easy to create tasty and healthful dishes while avoiding static foods. There is a tendency today, among people new to vegetarian cuisine, to load recipes with onions, garlic and strong spices so as to overwhelm the senses of the diner. However, another trend is on the rise which calls for the use of more subtle herbs and spices and innovative combinations of ingredients. This cookbook supports that trend.

Eat well, and enjoy a healthy, happy life.

The Editors

Introduction

When I first became a vegetarian, the only things I knew how to cook were frozen vegetables and macaroni and cheese. Gradually, I learned how to make bean stews and grain casseroles. Through the years, my kitchen ways have changed with the new foods or ideas I have discovered. My experiments turned the kitchen into a laboratory. Well-remembered are the year of the soybean, the month of agar gels, and Sunday night gluten dinners. The happy result of this experimenting is a basic knowledge of the various ingredients, and hence my style of cooking—alchemy!

After I have tried a recipe I rarely use it again except as a reference for certain proportions, such as baking powder-to-flour ratio. I personalize it by excluding items that my family doesn't eat. I include spices, add to the protein content, use leftovers, or take advantage of a bumper crop from the garden. Please do the same with the recipes in this book. Have fun with cooking; let it nurture your creativity as well as the health of those you love.

Vegetarian Lunches on the Run

When my children started school we were caught unprepared for packing lunch boxes. I didn't mind going to work with a baked squash under one arm, but little ones are subject to teasing and peer pressure. Even my husband was tired of squash on or off the cuff. The answer seemed to be sandwiches, but someone wouldn't eat bread and someone else said whole grains were hard to digest at a sit-down job. We began experimenting, asking friends, and thinking creatively to come up with new ideas. The results—packable, tasty, easy, healthful, reasonable-looking vegetarian lunches—I'm happy to share with you here.

Fast Foods and Do-Aheads

The best way to save time in the kitchen is to be organized. It really works. I used to make a large batch of soup base, put it into ice cube trays, transfer it to plastic bags in the freezer and then forget about it. A few months later I'd find these brown flecked cubes and I'd think that something had gone rotten. One day at my grandfather's house, I noticed a list on his freezer door. Frozen foods were listed under their categories, along with a shelf number and date of entry. I went home and organized the freezer and the pantry, too. Things rarely get lost now. Organization allows the cook to shop less and to move quickly in the kitchen. Making food in large batches, storing and portioning it saves trips to the garbage cans and compost pile.

Many recipes can be doubled and half frozen for another time. This is good to do with beans, especially chickpeas (garbanzos) which are handy little guys. Potatoes are grainy after freezing and no one likes them much. Fruit in season is cheaper and tastes better; freeze it for use out of season. In-season is a good time to can, freeze or dry batches of fruit leather, conserves, chutneys and sauces. Put things up in small containers and avoid waste; anything not eaten the first day after opening seems to go into an "untouchable" class.

Sometimes I keep bags of roasted soy flour (called *kino-goshi*), chickpea flour or dry burger mix in the refrigerator to preserve their nutrients and keep them fresh. Toasting and roasting seeds, nuts, and soybeans can be done once a week in a few minutes as can sprouting, making yogurt, and with more time, bread baking. Some people can do all this once a week; I rotate, doing one for a few weeks, then another. Having the kitchen and foods in order does save time.

When I get up in the morning, I don't expect to prepare gourmet lunch baskets from scratch. Rather, I assemble lunches while amusing the baby in his high chair, looking for lost socks, and putting out breakfast possibilities. Most of us do experience a morning time crunch; having readily available ingredients made ahead is important when you want to provide more than peanut butter-and-jelly on the run.

Leftovers

When I cook supper, I think about lunches for the next day and design the meal so that I can use its components for lunches. For example, Split Pea Soup is a good supper if we've been out skating, and in the morning I heat it up for lunch thermoses. Sometimes someone will want it for breakfast, too. Even if supper is just a salad, I make it big enough so that the next morning it can be thrown in a pot and simmered with broth or tomato sauce. Voila! Minestrone soup, in the time it takes to braid two heads of hair. Many of the recipes here use leftovers.

About packaging

I packed lunches in empty yogurt and cottage cheese containers until one day I noticed how inelegant and unappetizing it looked. I started thinking about how airlines handle moveable meals (all those little dishes), and decided that a horizontal lunch looked better than a vertical one. Horizontal also lets you choose the order in which to eat your food. This was a major breakthrough. The next obvious step is the palette effect. A dab of cranberry sauce sure brightens up fried tofu, and several pale green leaves from last night's artichokes would look nice next to a few black olives.

A spoonful of toasted sesame seeds sprinkled over a lunch freshens it up. A tablespoon of chutney would be a nice flavor in juxtaposition to the curried rice and vegetables. Orange carrot sticks add some color and raw crunch to a lunch of burger and applesauce. Somehow an impromptu salad appears and leftovers get used before they hit the slimy oblivion at the back of the refrigerator. Lunch has flavor, colors, textures, and variety, all of which get the digestive juices going.

Children enjoy separate little packages (have you ever seen what happens to lunch boxes in the cloak room?). Kept separate, the foods don't get soggy or discolored. Dipping into little containers is fun, and small packages are tradable.

We tried discouraging trading, but settled for a lecture on nutrition and hoped for the best. Our daughter was taking toasted sunflower seeds, peanuts, and fruit leather to school every day for months. I found out later that she was trading with everyone at her table for their carrots (she wanted to be able to see in the dark). This year she started asking for corn chips every day. When confronted with their dubious nutritional value she explained, "Oh, I don't eat them, but Gretchen's mother sends her the most delicious plums." We decided that trading isn't so bad.

Sometimes I buy pre-packaged items such as a case of little bottled juices, a box of fruit leathers, or applesauce in baby food jars (take off the labels to prevent teasing) to save some time. Bought in large quantities they can be economical.

Your choice of containers may be dependent upon your resources. For example, you may need to consider if you can fit your lunch into the tiny office refrigerator, if you'll be heating it up in a microwave or conventional oven, and if you can afford to occasionally lose a plastic container to the school lunchroom.

INTRODUCTION

About the foods in this cookbook

You may be unfamiliar with some of the items called for in these recipes. Don't let that stop you; substitute, or better yet, get to know how to use these healthy, delicious alternatives. Where possible, I have listed mailorder sources in the back of the book.

Agar or kuzu: a seaweed, often sold in powder form, that forms a jell-like food. It's tasteless by itself but takes on the flavor of other ingredients.

Arrowroot: A natural thickener which can be used like cornstarch or tapioca powder.

Chapatis: Flat, unleavened bread tortillas, homemade or found at the Indian or health food grocery.

Chili oil: Hot! Available in oriental markets.

Filo (phyllo): A pastry dough that is extremely thin and layered (this is what the Greek pastry baklava is made with). It's difficult and time consuming to make, but can be purchased in the grocery freezer section. Thoroughly defrost before trying to work with it.

Gluten flour: The protein part of wheat, free of starch and bran. Gluten, also called *seitan* (see recipes, page 108), which is made from this flour, is often used as a meat-like substitute and can be purchased in the refrigerated case at the health food store.

Hing: Also called asafetida. A dried resin from the Ferul plant (related to fennel). It is commonly used in East Indian cooking as a substitute for onion and/or garlic. It has a powerful, sometimes noxious smell when raw. The taste in cooked food resembles shallot or garlic. Use the yellow Cobra brand found in Indian or Middle Eastern grocery stores or supermarkets with international foods sections. One small container lasts months.

Lavash: a Middle Eastern type of flour tortilla. Available at Middle Eastern groceries or in the international foods section of some large supermarkets.

Nori: A seaweed that comes in flat sheets. Can be purchased at health food groceries or oriental markets

Miso: A fermented soybean paste, high in protein, helpful bacteria and B vitamins, used as a seasoning. Dissolve it first in a small amount of hot water; do not boil. Can be purchased at health food groceries or oriental markets.

Nutritional yeast: Yellow flakes that are very high in B vitamins. Nutritional yeast is different from brewer's yeast (which has a different look also—brownish granules); the latter has a bitter taste. Can be purchased at health food groceries.

Pita bread: Flat, round unleavened bread. When you cut it in half, you get two "pockets". Can be purchased at your local grocery.

Spring roll wrappers: Thin flour wafers; available in oriental markets in the refrigerator or freezer section, or in the produce section of your supermarket.

Tahini: A butter made from crushed sesame seeds. It's a good binder and has a creamy, nutty flavor. It is more smooth and flowing than sesame butter, so it's not a good idea to substitute. Can be purchased at health food groceries.

Tamari: An aged soy sauce made from soybeans, salt and water. Some are made with wheat, some are wheat free. It has a richer taste than regular soy sauce. Can be purchased at health food groceries, oriental markets, or in the international foods section of your supermarket.

Tofu: A soy food made from curdling soybean milk and pressing the curds into cakes. Tofu is a high protein food which is bland in taste but can be added to recipes, fried, and spiced. It should be kept in the refrigerator in a tub of water. Used in recipes, it can be left at room temperature for several hours. Can be purchased in the produce section of most supermarkets, at health food groceries or oriental markets. Different styles are available; generally, soft style is good for sauces and blending, while hard style is better for frying.

Wasabi powder: Powdered horseradish root; available in oriental groceries.

Yuba: When soymilk is heated and cooled, it forms a skin on the top. The Japanese lift this off and dry it as a highly concentrated form of protein. Can be purchased at an oriental market.

About dairy products

Not all of us can tolerate dairy products. The recipes in this book calling for milk can be made with soymilk, nut milk or calcium drink. Cream may be substituted with less water, more nuts and a bit of margarine when making nut milk.

About non-dairy or low-fat alternatives

Alternative ingredients can be found in brackets [like this]. These alternatives will lower the fat and/or reduce or eliminate the dairy products in the recipe.

About spices

The recipes in this book are usually gently seasoned and are adaptable to personal preferences.

Community Farms

I would like to put in a word here about community farms. My community has one and I have found it to be a wonderful thing. About seventy families support "the farm" (it is really three separate farms that work together). The way ours works is that each family gives a monthly pledge according to capacity or conscience or average use. Two times a week we have "store hours" when produce and milk can be picked up. Not only do we all get fresh vegetables and milk organically grown but we are also learning to eat seasonally. The farmers can work without worry for money, which in itself is a wonderful thing in a time of folding small family farms. And finally, the consumers are put in a position of knowing their farmer and being in touch with the land and weather.

On a typical Saturday morning people fill their paper bags from bins of fresh vegetables, remarking to one another how the green bean crop is terrific because of all that rain last month, or exchanging recipes for dealing with zucchini baseball bats and cooing at backpacked babies. In one corner a group of young mothers is organizing babysitting for a weeding party while in another corner a farmer is discussing milk production with another member. The children range around in groups, their mouths orange from munching carrots, while they visit and name the newest calf. Someone brings in flowers and now there are posies tucked in among the shoppers' vegetables. The bulletin board is full of ads for honey, apartments, sheepskins, directions to the farms' blueberry orchards or notices about upcoming farm festivals.

For information about community farms, write to our farmer:

Anthony Grahm
Echo Farm RFD #1
Wilton, NH 03086

Chapter 1

Breads, Wrappers & Sandwich Ideas

Table of Contents

CHAPTER ONE: BREADS

My first home-baked loaf of bread was a disaster because I didn't know the difference between baking yeast and brewer's yeast. Shortly thereafter I found the *Tassajara Bread Book*—an excellent resource. I have also found the *Cornell Bread Book* useful with its information on protein complementing. I have included only a few of our favorite or unusual breads here. There are many books of fine recipes for breadbaking; I encourage you to try it.

One way out of the boring lunch syndrome is to start thinking about the different forms bread can take, and even about omitting it from a sandwich altogether. One of my children's favorite lunches is what they call "toasted cheese without the bread." It is simply cheese melted on a pan and scooped up with chopsticks! I can't remember how this strange treat evolved.

You can scoop the seed cavity out of tomatoes, peppers, and cucumbers and fill. Apples and bananas (kept fresh by first dipping them in citrus juice) or cucumbers can be cut in slices with fillings sandwiched between. Raw zucchini, winter squash or turnips can be used also. Cabbage leaves (steam-wilted) and nori seaweed can be used to wrap up fillings. There are many grain and non-grain foods that can be used in place of bread for sandwiches. Experiment!

Ideas for sandwich wrappers

muffins
rolls
bagels
matzohs
wontons
croissants
tortillas
crepes
pancakes
bread sticks
crackers
chapatis
rice cakes
oat cakes
waffles
sweet breads
steamed breads
pocket breads (pita)
spring rolls
sliced vegetables
vegetable leaves
fruits
seaweed

Baking Powder Skillet Bread

We like to make this bread on camping trips to eat with hot Gluten (p. 108) or Hearty Stew (p. 59). In lunches, spread with spiced apple butter or cut open like biscuits and pour hot savory vegetables or Tofu in Gravy (p. 70) over them.

2 cups flour

2 pinches salt

2 pinches baking soda

2 teaspoon baking powder

1/2 cup yogurt

1/4 cup water

1. Mix dry ingredients, mix wet ingredients, and then mix both together.

2. Divide the dough into four pieces. Pat these each into flat circles 1/2 inch thick.

3. Cut the circles in quarters (you now have 16 triangles).

4. Cook these in an oiled skillet on medium heat, 10 minutes on each side.

Boston Brown Bread

When cool, this bread can be sliced thinly to make great sandwiches: baked bean and cream cheese or baked bean and spicy mayonnaise. It can be toasted with butter for breakfast too, and freezes well.

1. Stir all ingredients together and fill greased cans 2/3 full (or use oiled straight-sided quart or pint glass canning jars). Cover with foil held on with a rubber band.

2. Place jars on a trivet waist-deep in water and bring to a boil. Simmer covered for 1 hour (to 3 hours if you use 2 pound cans).

3. Cool, remove from jars or cans and slice.

1 cup cornmeal

1 cup rye flour

1 cup whole wheat flour

1 teaspoon baking soda

1 teaspoon baking powder

1 teaspoon salt

1/4 cup oil or melted butter
   (optional)

1/2 cup black strap or 3/4
   cup regular molasses

1 1/2 cups milk [or soy
   milk]

1/2 cup yogurt

1/2 cup dates or raisins
   (optional)

2 1/2 cups bran
1 1/2 cups whole wheat
   flour
2 Tablespoons oil
1/4 cup molasses
1 cup shredded carrots
1 cup currants or raisins
1 1/2 cups apple juice
1 teaspoon ground
   cinnamon
1/2 teaspoon ground
   ginger
1/2 teaspoon ground cloves

Branny Bran Muffins

1. **Mix together.**

2. **Spoon 2/3 full into greased muffin tins. Bake at 350°
for 1/2 hour.**

Bread Sticks

If you happen to be baking bread, you can easily make up a
bunch of these (or let the kids; although they tend to get
over creative, they'll eat what they make).

1. **Make bread with a standard bread recipe.**

2. **Roll dough into long ropes 1/2 inch in diameter. Cut
into desired lengths and roll them in sesame or poppy
seeds.**

3. **Cover loosely with a damp cloth and allow to rise 15-
20 minutes.**

4. **Bake at 350° until golden brown.**

Cream Cheese Wafers

1. Mix flour and spices. Cut butter and cream cheese in.

2. Form large balls and roll out into 1 inch diameter snakes.

3. Refrigerate 1 hour or until you wish to use. The dough keeps in the refrigerator up to two weeks. It can also be frozen.

4. To use, slice thinly and bake on ungreased cookie sheet at 350° for 8 minutes or until done.

2 cups flour
1/8 teaspoon salt
pinch paprika
1 stick of butter, softened
3 ounces cream cheese,
   softened

Croissants

You can make your own croissants, but I buy them to save time. Kept frozen until needed, they can be thawed before using.

1. Break in half. Scoop out some of the middle to make hollow horns.

2. Stuff (the halves are not rejoined). See Chapter Two for filling ideas.

Dilled Cottage Cheese Bread

2 Tablespoons yeast
1/4 cup honey
1 1/2 cups warm water
4 Tablespoons butter [or
   margarine]
2 cups cottage cheese
5 cups flour (approximately)
2 teaspoons salt
1/4 cup dill seed

1. Mix together yeast, honey and warm water and set aside until yeast blooms (rises in a thick foam to the surface of the liquid), 5-10 minutes.

2. Melt butter or margarine with cottage cheese in saucepan. When cool, add to yeast mix.

3. Add flour, salt and dill and knead all together well, adding enough flour to get a nice soft dough.

4. Let sit covered in a warm place in an oiled bowl for 1/2 hour. Punch down. Let rise 20 minutes.

5. Knead and divide in half. Shape loaves and bake at 350° for 45 minutes or until done.

Filo Sandwiches

Buy frozen packaged filo or make your own.

1. **Cut 2 sheets of filo leaves into 4 inch wide strips.**

2. **Brush with melted butter or margarine. Place filling (see Chapter Two) in one corner and fold in triangle fashion (like folding a flag) the length of the strip.**

3. **Brush outside with butter, sprinkle with sesame or poppy seeds and bake at 350° until golden.**

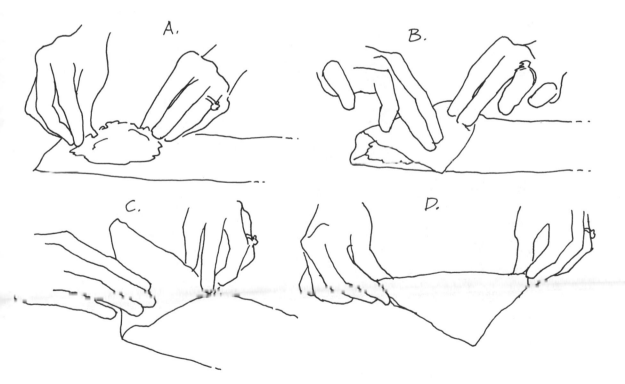

Garbanzo Chips

Some like these with Tofu Tartar Sauce (p. 158), others with spicy sauces.

4 cups water

1 teaspoon salt

2 cups garbanzo flour
   (pulverize raw chickpeas
   in a blender or food
   processor until fine)

1. Whisk all together and stir over medium heat until the mixture thickens sufficiently to gather in a lump and pull away from the sides of the pot.

2. Stuff into juice cans or wide mouth quart-size mason jars. When cooled all through, this can be sliced 1/4 inch thick and fried.

Gaspe Bread

1. In a bowl, mix honey, yeast and water. Let sit until the yeast blooms, 5-10 minutes.

2. Add butter and salt, mashed potatoes and 1 cup flour. Stir very, very well. Add the remaining flour (enough to get earlobe consistency).

3. Knead well and turn into a greased bowl; cover. Let rise in a warm place for 1/2 hour or more.

4. Divide in two, knead and shape in round baking pans. Let rise 20 minutes more.

5. Bake at 350° for 45 minutes or until golden.

3 Tablespoons honey
1 1/2 cups warm water
2 Tablespoons baking yeast
3 Tablespoons butter [or margarine]
1 Tablespoon salt
6 cups flour
1 cup potatoes (left over, mashed)

Nests

Nests are crisp little hollow forms that hold fillings.

Bread Nests

1. Cut the crusts from a piece of bread (save for making burgers).

2. With a rolling pin, roll out the bread slightly.

3. Butter or margarine both sides lightly and push into a muffin tin. Repeat for more nests.

4. Bake at 300° until golden and crisp.
Send filling in a thermos and fill the nest at eating time (the nests will get soggy if prefilled; they store well for two days).

Potato Nests

1. Shred a raw peeled potato, drain.

2. Heat deep oil to 400°.

3. In a large stainless tea strainer, arrange an overlapping layer of potato shreds. Place a smaller tea strainer inside to hold the shreds in place while frying.

4. Fry until golden, cool and remove. These can be stored for two days.

Noodle Nests

Follow directions for Potato Nests, using cooked noodles in place of potato shreds.

Potato Skin Nests

1. Split a raw potato in half. Scoop out the middle, leaving a 1/2 inch wall all around.

2. Boil for about 10 minutes and drain

3. Deep fry until golden in 400° oil.

Alternate:
Use leftover baked potato with the middle scooped out (these don't need frying).

Tortilla Nests

Fry corn tortillas like Potato Nests or poke into muffin tins and bake about 10 minutes at 350°.

Oatcakes

Try these with butter and jam or apple butter and thin slices of cheddar cheese.

1 1/2 cups oatmeal
(process rolled oats in a
blender or food
processor)
1/8 teaspoon baking soda
2 pinches salt
1 Tablespoon melted butter
[or margarine]
1/3 cup hot water
(approximately)

1. Mix dry ingredients. Pour melted butter over and slowly add enough hot water to form a thick dough.

2. Flour rolling pin and bread board with oat flour and roll out circles 1/8 inch thick.

3. Cut into quarters and bake at 350° for 20 minutes or cook on an ungreased skillet 10 minutes each side.

Pizza Turnovers

For the crust, use puff pastry or a pie crust dough.

1. Roll out the dough to a little more than 1/8 inch thick.

2. Cut in 5 inch squares.

3. Fill with grated cheese, tomato sauce, and whatever vegetables you like.

4. Fold over and crimp edges.

5. Bake at 350° until golden.

Pratie Oaten (Irish oaten potato cakes)

The kids like pratie oaten with hot Welsh Rarebit (p. 138) poured over them (the pratie oatens).

1. Combine the potatoes, salt, pepper and oatmeal, adding enough milk to make a thick dough.

2. Roll out 1/4 inch thick and cut into rounds. Fry in butter or bake on a hot skillet.

*2 1/2 cups mashed
   potatoes (leftovers)*
1 teaspoon salt
pinch pepper
*3 cups oatmeal (grind oats
   in a blender or food
   processor to make a very
   coarse flour)*
milk
butter [or margarine]

Puff Pastry Turnovers

You can buy this frozen, either in sheets or in little cup shapes. The cup shapes can be baked and filled. The flat sheets can be defrosted, rolled larger and cut into squares and folded over filling into a tringle. Crimp edges and bake at 350° until golden.

For fillings, try:

Chili con veg (p. 54)

Pot pie filling (p. 118)

Gluten in gravy (p. 64)

*Spicy Mexican vegetables
    (p. 68)*

*Spicy Indian vegetables
    (p. 67)*

Puris

The first time I ever saw these was at a border crossing between Nepal and India. A young man with a pile of these would pick one up, poke an indentation in it with his thumb, scoop some filling into it, and pop it into a very fat official's mouth. All with his right hand and all repeated whenever the official grunted. I boxed these up whole and we enjoyed playing this scene on a long car trip. I held the tray on my lap to avoid spills and filled the mouths of the grunters.

For fillings, try:

Peach Chutney (p. 152)

*Spanish Hazelnut Sauce
    (p. 156)*

Hummus (p. 41)

1. Mix and add enough water to make a flabby dough.

2. Shape into 3/4 inch balls and roll out into 2 inch circles.

3. Drop into hot oil. They puff out into balls and turn golden when done.

*1 cup unbleached or whole
    wheat pastry flour*

1/2 teaspoon baking soda

dash salt

Sandwich Logs

My youngest child is very fond of these. She says that they are also valuable trade items. These can be eaten as a log or sliced into 1 inch thick slices.

1. Cut the crusts off a slice of bread.

2. Roll out with a rolling pin and spread with any filling the consistency of softened cream cheese. Roll up into a log.

Sesame Pancakes

Pack a dip or spread to go on these. This recipe is a good source of calcium. It contains no wheat or dairy products, and is a complementary protein source to a soy spread.

1. Process rye and water in a blender or food processor.

2. Stir in remaining ingredients.

3. Fry on an oiled skillet on medium low heat. Flip when golden brown.

1 cup rolled rye (oats are okay)
4 cups water
1 cup millet flour (whiz millet in a blender until flour)
1 cup sesame seed meal (whiz in a blender until flour)
1/2 teaspoon salt

Steamed Sweet Bread

This bread makes a nice cream cheese and/or peanut butter sandwich. Like the Boston Brown Bread (p. 13), the kids really like these rounds broiled with a little butter on them for breakfast.

1. Combine wet ingredients and dry ingredients separately.

2. Mix and fold in chopped items.

3. Oil medium-sized cans, or straight-sided glass canning jars. Fill 2/3 - 3/4 full of batter and cover with aluminum foil held on with a rubber band. Place on a trivet in a pot of waist-deep water on the stove.

4. Bring to a boil, reduce heat and steam, covered, for 1 hour.

5. Remove and cool. Slide a knife around insides of jars to slide out the bread. Slice in rounds.

Dry ingredients:

1/2 cup soy flour

1 1/2 cups whole wheat
   flour

1 cup corn meal

1 teaspoon salt

1 1/2 teaspoons baking
   powder

1/2 teaspoon cinnamon

Wet ingredients:

3/4 cup molasses or
   honey

1 cup water

1/2 cup yogurt

Chopped ingredients:

1/2 cup grated carrots

1/2 cup chopped dates

1/4 cup chopped walnuts

Strollers

1. Slice a piece of pita bread in half horizontally to make 2 thin flat rounds.

2. Place filling in these with shredded vegetables and roll up.

3. Roll these in waxed paper, tucking ends in as you roll. To eat, just peel down from top as you go.

Tortillas

These can be cooked in the following two ways to make a dipping chip or an edible plate. We like these best as tostadas with chopped raw vegetables, refried beans, grated cheese and sour cream (pack in containers to be spooned out at lunch).

Fried

In a skillet, put a little butter or oil or margarine. Fry tortilla on both sides to desired crispness. Drain on paper towels.

Baked

Bake at 350° until crisp, about 5 minutes.

Vegetable Braid

If you happen to be baking bread, you can set aside a soft ball-sized lump of dough for a vegetable braid.

1. When the dough has gone through one rising, roll it out to 1/2 inch thick rectangle.

2. Make slits along the sides.

3. Fill with one of the more solid and flavorful fillings.

4. Fold sides in, overlapping each other. Bake at 350° for 45 minutes.

Yeasty Crepes

These evolved when a friend had phlebitis and needed to get a lot of B vitamins. I loved them when I was pregnant for the same reason.

1. Combine the dry ingredients and add enough water to make a thin batter.

2. Pour a small crepe-size amount onto a hot oiled skillet.

3. Cook until set, flip and quickly cook other side.

4. Roll them up on site with a filling of spicy vegetables, or add spice (a pinch each of cinnamon, ground cloves and nutmeg) to the batter and roll up with ricotta cheese, raisins and pecans for a filling.

1 cup nutritional yeast
1 cup whole wheat pastry
  flour
1 cup water
  (approximately)

Zwieback

A child can suck on these on long car trips to alleviate car sickness (also helps Mom with morning sickness) as there aren't any fats or oils as in most crackers.

1. Slice bread (or use presliced) about 1/2 inch thick.

2. Bake in a slow oven, about 200°-250° 1 hour, or until toasted all through. When cool, store in airtight container. Keeps very well.

Sandwich Suggestions

❦ Apple butter and mild cheddar cheese on oatmeal bread

❦ Asparagus spears and Tofu Mayonnaise (p. 158) in a Sandwich Log (p. 25)

❦ Avocado and Pan Fried Tofu (p. 115) on Skillet Bread (p. 12)

❦ Avocado, Spicy Vegetables (pp. 67 & 68), and mayonnaise in Croissant Horns (p. 15)

❦ Avocado and powdered pecans in Sandwich Logs (p. 25)

❦ Baked beans and cream cheese on Boston Brown Bread (p. 13)

❦ Baked beans, dijon mustard, and Tofu Mayonnaise (p. 158) on Boston Brown Bread (p. 13)

❦ Brown Gluten (p. 108) and sauerkraut on matzoh

❦ Brown Gluten (p. 108), lettuce, tomato, and mayonnaise on rye

❦ Burger (p. 96), mayonnaise, tomato, lettuce, pickle, ketchup, and mustard on a sesame seed bun

❦ Cashew butter and Spicy Vegetables (pp. 67 & 68) in Puris (p. 24)

❦ Cream cheese and chopped green olives on oatmeal bread

❦ Cream cheese and chopped pineapple on Steamed Sweet Bread (p. 26)

❦ Cream cheese and Peach Chutney (p. 152) on waffles

❦ Cream cheese and fresh chopped herbs in Sandwich Logs (p. 25)

❦ Cream cheese and Marinated Vegetables (p. 81) on rice cakes

❦ Cream cheese and pecans on pancakes

31

❦ Cream cheese, Mama Papa's Peppers (p. 80), and black olives on tortillas

❦ Cream cheese, mashed avocado, and Lemon Honey Jelly (p. 149) on matzohs

❦ Cream cheese on Steamed Sweet Bread (p. 26) or Vegetable Braid (p. 28)

❦ Feta cheese and chopped pecans in Sandwich Logs (p. 25)

❦ French Toast (p. 106) or waffles with Lemon Honey Jelly (p. 149)

❦ Gluten (p. 108) cooked in Sea Broth (p. 64) with tartar sauce in a pita Stroller (p. 27)

❦ Golden Tofu Nuggets (p. 109), lettuce, tomato, and mayonnaise wrapped in a pita Stroller (p. 27)

❦ Golden Tofu Nuggets (p. 109) and Lemon Honey Jelly (p. 149) on crackers

❦ Grated cheese, mayonnaise and chopped raw cauliflower on Garbanzo Chips (p. 18)

❦ Guacamole on corn chips

❦ Honey Fried Tofu (p. 110) and spicy Tofu Mayonnaise (p. 158) in pita Strollers (p. 27)

❦ Hummus (p. 41) and Mama Papa's Peppers (p. 80) on rice cakes

❦ Hummus (p. 41), sprouts and tomato on pita bread

❦ Mashed curry-spiced Mung Bean Spread (p.41), Peach Chutney (p. 152), and sour cream in Puris (p. 24)

❦ Mashed Lentil Spread (p. 41) with Mama Papa's Peppers (p. 80), avocado, and parmesan cheese on rice cakes

❦ Mashed Mung Bean Spread (p. 41) with Marinated Cauliflower (p. 81) and Curry Butter (p. 148), rolled in chapatis (p. 5)

❦ Nut Loaf (p. 137) and mayonnaise on Oatcakes (p. 22)

❦ Pan Fried Tofu (p. 115), tartar sauce with capers on matzoh

❦ Pan Fried Tofu (p. 115), mayonnaise, and tomato on rye bread

❦ Peanut butter and apple butter in Sandwich Logs (p. 25)

❦ Peanut butter and cheese slices on oatmeal bread

❦ Peanut butter and cooked mashed parsnips on Steamed Sweet Bread (p. 26)

❦ Peanut butter and cream cheese rolled in Yeasty Crepes (p. 29)

❦ Peanut butter and D.V.'s Mincemeat (p. 146) on Boston Brown Bread (p. 13)

❦ Peanut butter, chopped celery, and mayonnaise on bagels

❦ Peanut butter, roasted almonds, chopped celery, and mayonnaise on Steamed Sweet Bread (p. 26)

❦ Peanut butter, Tofu Mayonnaise (p. 158), grated carrots, and raisins on muffins

❦ Peanut butter, Yellow Gluten (p. 108), and Peach Chutney (p. 152) on chapatis (p. 5)

❦ Pesto Sentio (p. 153) and tomato in Croissant Horns (p. 15)

❦ Refried Bean Spread (p. 42), Mama Papa's Peppers (p. 80), and black olives on corn bread

❦ Refried Bean Spread (p. 42), tomato slices, grated jack cheese, and sour cream in a Tortilla Nest (p. 21)

❦ Sliced cooked beets and Tofu Mayonnaise (p. 158) on Gaspe Bread (p. 19)

❦ Sliced cucumbers and Tofu Mayonnaise (p. 158) on oatmeal bread

❦ Sliced tomatoes and Herb Butter (p. 148) on matzohs

❦ Sliced tomatoes and Tofu Mayonnaise (p. 158) in pita pockets

❧ **Split Pea Spread (p. 41), spicy Tofu Mayonnaise (p. 158) and black olives on corn bread**

❧ **Split Pea Spread (p. 41), Tahini Dip (p. 44), tomato and sprouts in pita pockets**

❧ **Sunflower seeds, mayonnaise, and mashed artichoke hearts in Croissant horns (p. 15)**

❧ **Sunflower seeds, mayonnaise, grated cheese, and tomato on Oatcakes (p. 22)**

❧ **Soy Scrapple (p. 127) and sauerkraut on croissant horns**

❧ **Tofu Tartar Sauce (p. 158), cheese slices, and cucumbers on crackers**

❧ **Yellow Gluten (p. 108) and Cranberry Ketchup (p. 143) in a tortilla**

Chapter 2

Fillings & Spreads

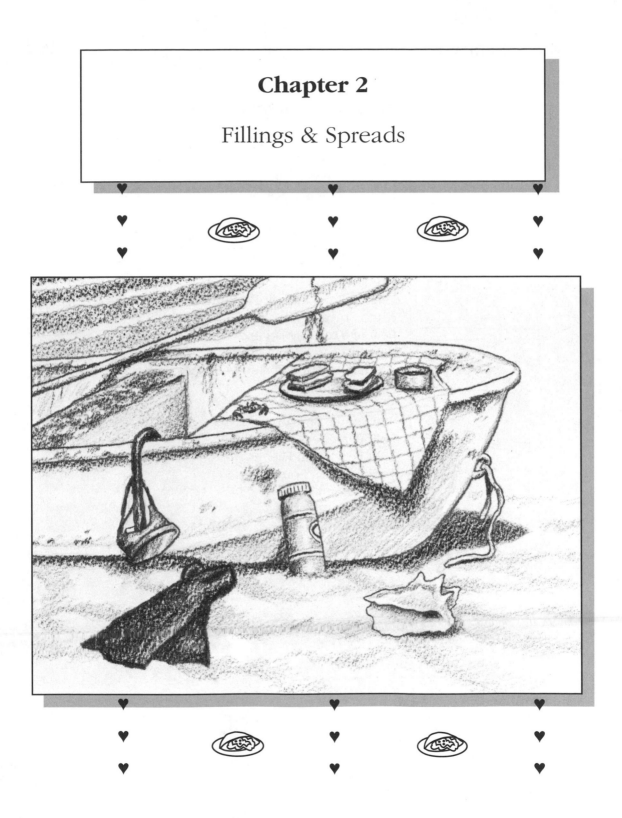

Table of Contents

CHAPTER TWO: FILLINGS & SPREADS

Fillings can be sandwiched or stuffed into wrappings or packed in a container to be eaten with chips or a spoon.

Artichoke Hearts Delight

These are delicious stuffed in croissant horns.

1. **Heat artichoke hearts in a saucepan.**

2. **Add the mayonnaise, cream and parmesan cheese.**

3. **Remove from heat and mash slightly.**

6 artichoke hearts
1/3 cup cream
1/2 cup Tofu Mayonnaise
   (p. 158)
2 Tablespoons parmesan
   cheese

Baba Ganov

This is delicious stuffed in fresh tomatoes, eaten on pita bread with sliced tomatoes, or dipped on dry rye crackers.

1. **Bake eggplant at 375° until skin blisters.**

2. **Peel, chop and mix with other ingredients.**

3. **Let sit overnight to meld the flavors.**

1 1/2 cups chopped baked
   eggplant
1 teaspoon salt
2 Tablespoons fresh chopped
   chives (optional)
5 Tablespoons lemon juice
3 Tablespoons chopped fresh
   parsley
pinch black pepper
3 Tablespoons olive oil
1/4 cup sour cream
   [or 1 Tablespoon tahini]

Cheddar Spread

This is good hot or cold. If you happen to be near a toaster oven, try some spread on an English muffin and broiled.

Variation:
Add 1 teaspoon fresh snipped dill weed or 2 Tablespoons chopped dill pickle.

1 cup grated cheddar cheese
1/2 cup Tofu Mayonnaise
    (p. 158)

Cheese Eggplant Spread

Delicious in a pita stroller or wrapped in lavash or a flour tortilla.

1. **Saute the cabbage and green peppers in olive oil.**

2. **Add the eggplant, salt, and hazelnuts. Cover and simmer gently until soft.**

3. **Cool for a minute or two and crush slightly while mixing in the grated cheese.**

1/4 head of cabbage,
    chopped
1 green pepper, chopped
1/4 cup olive oil
2 large eggplants, peeled and
    cubed
1 cup toasted hazelnuts,
    chopped
1 teaspoon salt or to taste
1 cup grated mild cheddar
    cheese

Chickpea Salad

1. Mash chickpeas and cream cheese together until all the chickpeas are at least broken in half.

2. Stir in the cottage cheese and celery. Season to taste.

3. Chill. Thin with milk if needed. To lighten richness, add more cottage cheese and less cream cheese.

Variation:
Add 1 Tablespoon curry powder; stir and chill.

3 cups cooked or canned chickpeas (garbanzos)
8 ounces cream cheese
1 cup cottage cheese
2 cups chopped celery
salt and pepper to taste

Chickpea Souffle Spread

Mix all ingredients together.

1 cup Chickpea Souffle (p. 99)
1/4 cup pine nuts
1/4 cup mayonnaise [Tofu Mayonnaise (p. 158)]
1/4 cup chopped celery
1/4 cup raisins (optional)

Creamed Honey Spread

When uncapped honey comes into contact with air, it crystallizes into a grainy texture. When whipped, hence oxygenated with the tiny crystals in the creamed honey, the new honey will grow tiny crystals rather than the coarse grainy ones, resulting in a creamy texture.

This makes a nice thick spread that can be spiced if desired and used with nut butters for a sandwich spread. (Save out a cup for making the next batch.)

1 cup prepared creamed
*   honey*
6 cups honey
*   (not crystallized)*

1. In a blender or with a mixer, combine until well blended.

2. Place in a covered container for a few weeks until very tiny crystals begin to grow. The crystals are so small that the honey will be creamy rather than grainy.

Fruit Spread

4 cups any mix of chopped
*   dried fruits (prunes,*
*   raisins, apricots, dates,*
*   peaches, apples, or*
*   pineapples)*
1/2 cup grated carrots
1 teaspoon salt
1/3 cup lemon juice
1 teaspoon grated lemon
*   rind*
1 1/2 cups water

1. Simmer all gently for 1 hour.

2. Cream together in a blender.

3. Simmer again until thick.

Hummus

This is usually eaten on pita bread, but it can also become a sauce on spicy vegetables.

Whip all ingredients in a blender or food processor.

*2 cups cooked or canned
   chickpeas (garbanzos)
1/2 cup tahini
2 Tablespoons lemon juice
1 teaspoon dill weed or
   cumin
salt to taste*

Lentil, Mung, or Split Pea Spread

1. Cook the legumes (in proportions: 1 cup legumes to 2 cups water) until soft, around 45 minutes. Drain off excess water.

2. Puree to the consistency of applesauce. Salt to taste.

*1 cup legumes
2 cups water
salt to taste*

Nutto Spread

Stir all ingredients together.

*1/2 cup Tofu Mayonnaise
   (p. 158)
1/2 cup cashew butter or
   tahini
1/2 cup finely chopped celery
1/2 cup chopped olives
1/2 cup chopped pecans*

Peanut Yeast Spread

1/2 cup peanut butter
1/2 cup Tofu Mayonnaise
   (p. 158)
1/4 cup nutritional yeast

This is a high protein spread. Good in a sandwich with tomatoes and sprouts.

Mix all ingredients together.

Refried Bean Spread

1/2 teaspoon cumin
pinch cayenne
1/4 teaspoon salt
1 cup pinto beans, cooked

Beans that have been cooked very soft can be gently mashed and simmered in an oiled skillet with cumin, salt, and cayenne till the beans loose moisture and firm up. When cool, they should be spreadable.

Sesame Avocado Spread

1/4 cup tahini
1 teaspoon tamari
3 Tablespoons hot water
juice of 1 lemon
1 avocado
1/4 teaspoon paprika

Keep this in a covered container until time to eat; air exposure browns avocado.

1. **Mix the tahini, tamari, water and juice.**

2. **Add the avocado and paprika and mash well.**

Sliced Sopnut

1. **Process all ingredients to a thick batter in a blender. If it is too thin, stir in a few teaspoons of texturized vegetable protein or whole wheat bread crumbs.**

2. **Pour into wide-mouth, straight-sided canning jars or 1 pound cans. Cover with foil and tie on.**

3. **Place jars on a trivet waist-deep in water in a covered pot. Steam for about 2 hours.**

4. **Remove and cool. Slice.**

1 cup peanut butter
1 cup tomato puree
1 cup soy flour
3/4 cup water
1 teaspoon hing
1 Tablespoon nutritional yeast
1/4 cup miso
1/4 cup arrowroot or cornstarch or powdered tapioca
1 teaspoon salt

Sopnut Spread

Mash Sopnut with mayonnaise and chopped pickle.

1 cup Sopnut (above)
1/2 cup Tofu Mayonnaise (p. 158)
1/4 cup chopped pickle

Soy Souffle Spread

Stir all ingredients together.

1 cup Soy Souffle (p. 128)
1/4 cup mayonnaise
1/4 cup toasted sunflower seeds
1/4 cup chopped celery

Split Pea Cheese Spread

1 cup cooked Split Pea Puree
   (p. 41)
1 cup grated mild cheddar
   cheese
1/2 cup spicy Tofu
   Mayonnaise (p. 158)

Combine. Makes good use of left over split pea soup. I prefer this spread hot.

Split Pea Tahini Dip

1 cup cooked Split Pea Puree
   (p. 41)
2 Tablespoons lemon juice
1/2 cup tahini
1 teaspoon soy sauce
1/8 cup grated parmesan
   cheese

Another great way to use left over split pea soup.

Stir all ingredients together. Serve hot or cold.

Tahini Cream Spread

6 ounces cream cheese,
   softened
2 - 3 Tablespoons tahini
dash of tamari
a little hot water for
   spreadability

This can be mixed with hot vegetables to melt in a thermos or as a spread. It can also be used in place of mayonnaise to moisten a vegetable or burger sandwich.

Mash all ingredients together.

Tofunut Spread

1. Mix water and peanut butter.

2. Add tofu and salt. Process in a blender or food processor.

3 Tablespoons boiling water
3 Tablespoons peanut butter
1/2 pound tofu
pinch salt

Tofu Pate

This is nice stuffed in croissants or spread on crackers.

Process all ingredients in blender or food processor and chill.

1 pound tofu
1 cup green beans
3 Tablespoons Tofu
*   Mayonnaise (p. 158)*
1/2 cup walnut meal
*   (make by processing*
*   walnuts in blender or food*
*   processor)*
1/2 teaspoon dijon-style
*   mustard*
2 pinches hing
3/4 teaspoon salt

Tofu Salad

This very simple spread is delicious, dairy-free and reminiscent of egg salad. This is my favorite sandwich filling.

Mix all ingredients together.

1 pound mashed tofu
1 cup Tofu Mayonnaise
*   (p. 158)*
1 cup chopped celery
salt and pepper to taste

Tomato Sunseed Spread

1 cup toasted sunflower seeds
1/2 cup tomato puree
2 drops chili oil
2 Tablespoons finely chopped
   green peppers
2 Tablespoons finely chopped
   black olives

1. Grind sunflower seeds in a blender.

2. Add tomato puree.

3. Stir in remaining ingredients and salt to taste.

Vegnut Spread

1 cup Tofu Mayonnaise
   (p. 158)
1 cup peanut butter
1/2 cup shredded carrots
1/2 cup finely chopped celery
1/2 cup finely minced green
   peppers

1. Mix mayonnaise and peanut butter.

2. Stir in vegetables.

Yeast Spread

1/2 cup Tofu Mayonnaise
   (p. 158)
1/4 cup nutritional yeast
1/4 teaspoon prepared
   mustard
3 Tablespoons chopped sweet
   pickles or relish
1 Tablespoon capers or
   pickled nasturtium pods

Stir all ingredients together.

Chapter 3

Soups & Thermos Items

Table of Contents

CHAPTER THREE: SOUPS & THERMOS ITEMS

On cold winter days, it's nice to have a hot lunch. Included here are some suggestions that sure beat the food usually available at school or work. A hot sauce (see Chapter Six) over an open-faced sandwich is another good warm-up for a cold day.

Almond Soup

1. Whiz milk and almonds together in a blender or food processor. The almonds will settle to the bottom.

2. In a saucepan, simmer until almonds are soft and remain suspended in the thickened milk.

3. Add remaining ingredients except sour cream. Stirring, simmer about 10 minutes.

4. Remove from heat and whisk in sour cream.

1 cup almonds
1 cup milk
1/8 cup butter [or margarine]
1/8 cup flour
3 cups water
1/4 teaspoon salt
1/4 teaspoon Bell's seasoning <u>or</u> mix of turmeric, cumin, parsley, sage, rosemary and thyme
1/4 cup sour cream

American Chop Suey

1. Make chili base. (p. 100; Chili Fingers)

2. Pour over noodles. Sprinkle with shredded jack cheese, if desired.

Boston Brown Beans

1/2 pound tofu
1 cup cabbage
1/2 cup oil
3 cups dried beans
   (navy pea beans or dried
   lima beans) soaked overnight and drained
1 cup water
1/2 cup tomato puree
1 Tablespoon salt
1 cup molasses
2 Tablespoons mustard
   powder

1. Saute cabbage and tofu in oil until tender.

2. Combine with remaining ingredients and bake, covered, in a slow oven for 4 hours or until tender. Add more liquid as needed.

Shortcut for pressure cooker:
1. Combine beans, water, molasses, and tomato puree in a pressure cooker.

2. Bring up to pressure and cook 1/2 hour.

3. Combine with other ingredients and bake in a bean pot or covered casserole at 250° for 1 - 1 1/2 hours or until tender.

Brown Gluten Stew

2 cups brown gluten in 2 1/2
   cups of its own broth
2 carrots, chopped
4 medium potatoes, chopped
2 stalks celery, chopped
1/2 cup peas
2 cups chopped cabbage
1/4 cup whole wheat flour

This is made with brown gluten, often available in health food stores. A recipe is on page 108.

1. Simmer the gluten until firm.

2. Add the vegetables. Continue simmering another half hour until tender.

3. Sprinkle the flour over all and stir it in. Simmer 5 minutes more, until thickened.

Cabbage Soup

1. Cook cabbage in the water until almost soft.

2. Separately mix up the milk, flour, and potatoes. Add to cabbage. Add butter. Simmer 5-10 minutes more.

3. Season to taste (under-salt because of the later addition of salty parmesan cheese).

4. Add the parmesan cheese to the thermos when packing.

1 cabbage, shredded
2 cups water
1 cup mashed potato
2 cups milk
2 Tablespoons flour
3 Tablespoons butter
  [or margarine]
1 cup grated parmesan
salt and pepper to taste

Calcium Drink

I invented this drink when I was a nursing mother and allergic to milk. The children started begging sips, and now it runs a close third behind hot chocolate or hot cinnamon milk for a winter warm up drink.

1. Simmer water, oats, salt and fennel 20 minutes.

2. Process all ingredients in a blender and drink warm. Shake thermos before drinking to stir up the settling sunflower seed pieces.

4 cups cold water
1/2 cup oats
pinch salt
pinch fennel seeds
1/2 cup sunflower seeds
2 Tablespoons - 1/4 cup
   honey (to taste)

Cheddar Soup

This soup could also be a sauce. Alternatively, leave out the green peppers and add 3 cups chopped spinach at the end and you have *dippers*, so named because of the strips of toast you dip in the spinach-cheese sauce to scoop it up.

1. Melt butter or margarine in a saucepan and saute green peppers.

2. Sprinkle on the flour and slowly add milk while continuing to stir over medium heat.

3. Simmer 5 minutes while stirring, then add cheese and seasonings and remove from heat.

Variation:
For Tomato Cheese Soup, add 2 cups chopped fresh tomatoes or 1 cup tomato puree before adding cheese.

4 Tablespoons butter
    [or margarine]
1 cup finely chopped green
    peppers
4 Tablespoons flour
5 cups milk
3 cups grated sharp cheddar
    cheese
salt and pepper to taste

3 cups cooked or canned
   pinto or kidney beans
1 cup tomato sauce
1/4 cup olive oil
2 cups chopped cabbage
2 cups corn
2 green peppers, chopped
1/2 cup texturized vegetable
   protein or finely chopped
   Brown Gluten
1 teaspoon chili powder
   (more or less to taste) or
   pinch cayenne and 1
   teaspoon cumin powder
salt to taste

2 large potatoes (red or
   white), scrubbed and
   chopped
3 cups corn kernels
1/2 cup chopped celery
   (include some leaves)
1 cup water
1 cup milk [or soy or nutmilk]
2 Tablespoons texturized
   vegetable protein
   (optional) or 1 cup
   chopped frozen tofu
2 Tablespoons butter
   [or margarine]

Chili Con Veg

1. Saute vegetables in oil in a heavy pot.

2. Add remaining ingredients and simmer 1/2 hour, adding more liquid if needed.

Corn Chowder

1. Simmer vegetables and texturized vegetable protein or chopped tofu in water in a covered pot. When almost tender, add milk, salt, pepper, and butter.

2. Simmer 10 minutes more. Some people like to replace half the milk with cream or add a couple of tablespoons of sour cream to make a richer chowder.

Cream of Any Vegetable Soup

This is one of my clean-the-fridge recipes (like minestrone and burgers). Sometimes I put a dollop of sour cream in it, or add fresh or dried herbs.

1. Boil vegetables.

2. Puree vegetables with milk. Set aside.

3. In a saucepan, melt butter; sprinkle in flour, then wisk in milk slowly as the mixture thickens to a cream sauce. Add to vegetable mixture.

4. Stir in cream and seasonings and simmer 5 minutes more.

Try these spices:

dill with predominantly yellow vegetables or potatoes

nutmeg with spinach, chard or beet greens

marjoram with zucchini, green beans, tomatoes

parsley with cabbage family

2 cups chopped vegetables
1/2 cup water
   (to boil vegetables)
1 Tablespoon butter
   [or margarine]
2 Tablespoons whole wheat
   flour
1/2 cup milk [or soy or nut
   milk]
1/2 cup cream [or yogurt]
salt and pepper to taste

Cup-A-Lasagna

The amounts in this recipe depend upon the size of your ther-moses. Just keep layering until the thermos is full.

flour tortillas

tomato sauce

grated cheese (mozzarella or mild cheddar)

grated parmesan

ricotta cheese

spinach (optional)

1. Break the flour tortillas into pieces the size of the thermos bottom.

2. Heat the sauce very hot.

3. Layer tortillas, cheeses and sauce (and optional spinach, which will wilt nicely). Cap quickly and by lunch time, you'll have a warm, melty lasagna.

Curried Potatoes

1. **Heat oil and add black mustard seeds. When they turn grey and start to jump, add remaining ingredients, stir and cover.**

2. **Simmer until potatoes are done.**

1/2 cup oil

1/2 teaspoon black mustard seeds

1 teaspoon cumin

1 1/2 teaspoons turmeric

1/2 teaspoon hing

1/2 teaspoon cayenne

1 teaspoon fennel seed

1 1/2 teaspoons salt

8 potatoes (red or white) cut in 1/2 inch cubes

1 cup water or coconut milk

Gravies

Dal Gravy

*2 cups yellow split peas,
   cooked and pureed
2 Tablespoons salt
4 Tablespoons curry powder*

*or in place of curry powder:
   1/4 teaspoon hing
   1 Tablespoon turmeric
   2 Tablespoons cumin
   1/2 teaspoon coriander
   pinch cayenne
   2 pinches mustard seed*

This is an interesting hot gravy poured over cooked vegetables or grains. Thin it for soup or soup base, or mix it with yogurt, dried fruits, nuts and fresh chopped vegetables to make an interesting salad.

Stir all the spices into the peas and simmer gently 20 minutes, adjusting the seasonings and adding extra water to desired consistency.

Martha's Vegetable Stock Gravy

*2 cups juice from cooked
   vegetables (carrots, celery,
   etc.)
3 Tablespoons whole wheat
   flour
3 Tablespoons butter
   [or margarine]*

1. Melt butter, add flour and stir with whisk while slowly adding vegetable stock.

2. Simmer until thick. Salt to taste.

Nut Gravy

1. Grind nuts in a blender or food processor until the meal is like coarse flour; add water.

2. Melt butter, add flour and brown slightly.

3. Add nut mixture.

4. Add salt and stir until thick.

1/4 cup cashews
1 Tablespoon hazelnuts
1/2 cup water
1 Tablespoon butter
 [or margarine]
1 Tablespoon flour
1/8 teaspoon salt

Hearty Stew

1. Chop the vegetables and saute 5 minutes in oil.

2. Add water and simmer until tender.

3. Add beans, flour, and seasonings, and simmer 10 minutes more.

2 carrots, chopped
4 medium potatoes, chopped
2 stalks celery, chopped
1/2 cup peas
2 cups chopped cabbage
1/4 cup oil
2 1/2 cups water, stock, or
 bean juice
2 cups kidney beans, cooked
1/4 cup whole wheat flour
1/4 cup tamari
salt and pepper to taste

Lentil Soup

1/4 cup olive oil
1 cup chopped cabbage
1 cup chopped green pepper
2 cups dried lentils
5 cups water or more
2 teaspoons cumin seed
1 carrot, grated
2 Tablespoons tamari
pinch pepper
salt to taste
grated parmesan - to sprinkle
    on individual
    servings

1. Saute cabbage and green peppers in olive oil.

2. When soft, add lentils, water and spices and simmer. Leftover soup can be made into Burgers (p. 96) or Pepper Pot Soup (p. 62), or can be frozen.

Minestrone Soup

"Minestrone" means various little bits. This is a wonderfully versatile soup. Use any vegetables, any beans, any pasta or grains. After an Italian supper, chop all the pasta (with sauce on it), the antipasto (with Italian dressing on it), and simmer together.

1. Simmer vegetables and pasta in water until almost tender.

2. Add remaining ingredients and simmer 10 minutes until done.

*1/2 cup each: carrots, peas,
    and potatoes*
2 stalks chopped celery
1/2 cup chopped cabbage
1 cup chopped spinach
*4 ounces pasta (of various
    shapes)*
2 cups water
1/2 cup chickpeas, cooked
1/2 cup kidney beans, cooked
2 Tablespoons olive oil
1 cup tomato puree
*1/4 cup grated parmesan
    cheese*
1/2 teaspoon marjoram
1/2 teaspoon thyme
salt and pepper to taste

Pepper Pot Soup

3 medium carrots, sliced
1 turnip, cubed
1 tomato, chopped
1 zucchini, chopped
2 cups water
1 Tablespoon fresh chopped
    parsley
1 cup cooked lentils, pureed
1/4 cup tamari or
    1 Tablespoon miso
salt to taste
lots of freshly grated black
    pepper

1. Simmer vegetables in water until tender.

2. Add lentils, tamari and spices. Simmer another 10 minutes, gently.

Rainbow Clouds

My children named this, originally because it was a different color each time I made it, depending on what vegetables I used. After the name, we started to try to put as many colors in as we could. The beets stain and my youngest poetically calls this "Pink Blossoms".

1. Melt butter. Add flour, then slowly whisk in milk.

2. When thick, stir in tofu and vegetables (except tomatoes). Cover and continue to cook on low heat 5 minutes more.

3. Season with salt and fold in tomatoes. Garnish with grated cheese.

4 Tablespoons butter
[or margarine]
2 Tablespoons flour
1/2 cup milk
[or soy or nut milk]
1 pound tofu
(kneaded 2 minutes)
2 cups corn
1 cup grated carrots
1 cup chopped spinach
1 cup chopped tomatoes
(optional) or chopped
cooked beets
grated cheese (optional)

Savory Broths

These can make the base for barley, millet, rice, vegetable or noodle soups. They are also used to cook and marinate gluten or tofu. The brown or yellow broths can be made into gravy by whisking in about 3 tablespoons flour and simmering until thick.

Brown Broth

5 cups water
1/4 cup oil
1/4 cup tomato puree
1/2 cup tamari
1 teaspoon salt
1/2 teaspoon parsley
grate of fresh black pepper

Simmer all ingredients together.

Yellow Broth

5 cups water
1/4 cup oil
1 teaspoon salt
1/2 teaspoon parsley
1/2 teaspoon sage
1/2 teaspoon thyme
1/2 teaspoon cumin
1/2 teaspoon turmeric
3 Tablespoons nutritional
    yeast

Simmer all ingredients together.

Sea Broth

4 cups water
1/4 cup chopped dulse
1 teaspoon salt
juice of 1 lemon
1 Tablespoon molasses
1/4 teaspoon tarragon

Simmer all ingredients together.

Vegetable Broth

Blend ingredients in a blender or food processor and simmer until tender.

2 carrots
3 stalks celery
1/2 green pepper
2 Tablespoons parsley
2 Tablespoons tamari
1 quart water
salt to taste

Scotch Broth

Pippi Longstocking thought barley was nasty. However, this is one of my kids' favorite cooked foods. I've seen them foraging in the fridge with friends after school, each with a spoon, eating it cold from the pot.

1. Simmer split peas, vegetables and barley until tender.

2. Stir. The split peas will dissolve into a pureed look. Add seasonings. Garnish with grated cheese.

2 cups green split peas, dried
1 turnip, cubed small
1 carrot, cut small
1 cup fresh peas
1 cup barley
1/4 cup tamari
1 teaspoon chopped parsley
2 Tablespoons butter
  [or margarine]
grated cheddar cheese
  (optional)
salt and pepper to taste

Shepherds Pie

This is a layered casserole that's always requested the next day for lunch thermoses.

Bake 20 minutes at 350°.

Bottom layer is Tofu in Gravy
*   (p. 70)*
Next is peas
Top with mashed potatoes

Sloppy Joes

Heat Chili Base (p. 100) and pour into a thermos. At lunch, pour out onto whole wheat roll or English muffin.

Spicy Indian Vegetables

1. **Simmer gently about 20 minutes in a covered pot.**

2. **Add more water or coconut milk, if necessary.**

3. **Stir in spinach at the end to wilt.**

1 head cauliflower, chopped
1/2 cup chopped cashews
2 cups spinach, chopped
1 cup winter squash, cubed
2 Tablespoons butter
*   [or margarine]*
2 Tablespoons curry powder
1/4 cup water
*   (or coconut milk)*
1/4 teaspoon salt

Spicy Mexican Vegetables

1. **Saute vegetables briefly in butter.**

2. **Add water and spices.**

3. **Cover and simmer gently for about 15 minutes, adding water if necessary.**

2 cups corn
1 cup chopped green pepper
1 cup chopped sweet red
  pepper
1 cup chopped cabbage
2 Tablespoons butter
  [or margarine]
1/4 cup water
1 Tablespoon chili powder
1/4 teaspoon salt
1/2 cup chopped black olives
  (optional)

Squash Cheese Soup

1. In a saucepan, melt butter and whisk in flour.

2. Slowly add milk or broth while stirring and simmer until thickened.

3. Stir in cheese, squash, and seasonings. Simmer 5 minutes more.

3 Tablespoons butter [or margarine]

3 Tablespoons whole wheat flour

2 cups milk [or vegetable stock]

1 cup grated sharp cheddar cheese

2 cups cooked winter squash, mashed

salt and pepper to taste

Tofu in Gravy

Tofu in Gravy is a useful filling by itself. Pour over noodles or send in a thermos to fill nests (p. 20).

4 Tablespoons butter
  [or margarine]
3 Tablespoons whole wheat
  flour
2 cups milk [or broth, or nut
  milk]
1 1/2 pounds tofu, mashed or
  cubed
1/4 cup tamari

1. In a saucepan, melt butter and whisk in flour.

2. Slowly add the milk while stirring over medium heat.

3. When thick, add tamari and tofu and simmer gently 5 minutes more.

Tofu-Noodle or Tortillini Soup

1. **Bring water to a boil.**

2. **Add remaining ingredients and simmer until noodles are done.**

3 cups water

2 Tablespoons chopped celery

1 Tablespoon chopped parsley

4 ounces linguini broken
    into 2 inch lengths (or use
    cheese tortillini)

1 pound tofu, chopped fine

1 Tablespoon nutritional
    yeast flakes

2 teaspoons butter
    [or margaine]

salt to taste

Tomato Bisque Soup

3 Tablespoons butter
  [or margarine]
3 Tablespoons flour
2 cups milk
2 cups tomato puree
1 teaspoon basil
2 cups left over cooked brown
  rice
1/2 cup grated parmesan
  cheese
salt and pepper to taste

1. In a saucepan, melt butter and whisk in flour.

2. Slowly add milk while stirring.

3. Simmer until thick.

4. Add tomato puree, basil, and brown rice. Simmer 5 minutes more.

5. Remove from heat, add the cheese and season.

Chapter 4

Salads & Salad Dressings

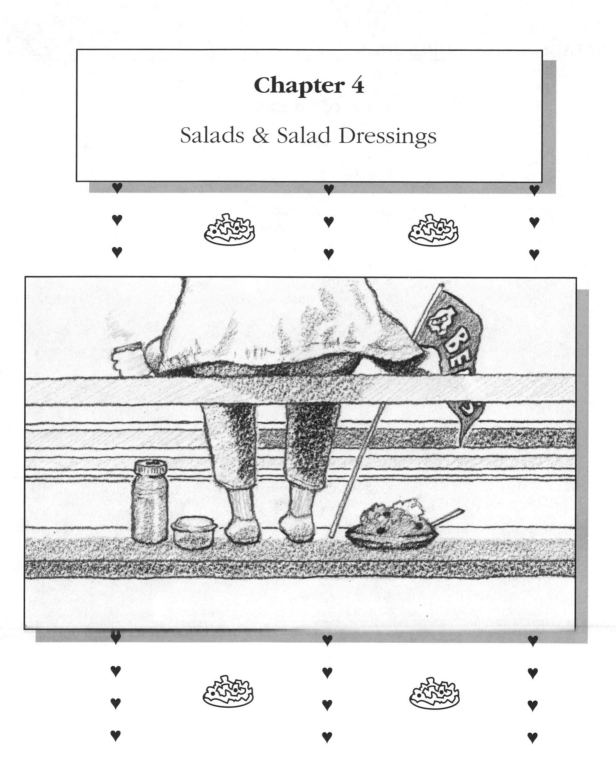

Table of Contents

CHAPTER FOUR: SALADS & SALAD DRESSINGS

Salads are getting more difficult to identify these days. Usually they are served cold, often with dressings and sometimes something raw. From there anything can be imagined.

Try cooked vegetables, marinated vegetables, raw vegetables, potatoes, pasta, grains, beans, sprouts, cheeses, fruits and tofu. Jellied salads are fun to make, pretty to look at, and delicious. Raw foods are some of the most important components of our diet, so salads deserve some attention, creativity, and plenty of space at every meal.

Many of the recipes in this chapter do not include exact amounts; you may vary these according to your taste and what you have on hand.

Artichoke Salad Cups

1. Steam artichokes for 50 minutes (or 10 minutes in a pressure cooker).

2. Gently pull back leaves enough to pull out central white thin low leaves and remove choke.

3. Fill with Tofu Salad (p. 45), Chickpea Salad (p. 39), Hummus (p. 41), or Guacamole (p. 79).

Carrot Salad

Stir dressing into other ingredients.

grated carrots
raisins
sour cream or yogurt or
    Tofu Mayonnaise (p. 158)
    or a combination

Coleslaw

Add the dressing to the grated cabbage. If desired, stir in grated carrot or pineapple or raisins.

grated cabbage
grated carrot (optional)
raisins or chopped pineapple
(optional)
sour cream or
Tofu Mayonnaise (p. 158)
or yogurt or a combination

Brussels Sprout Salad

Stir all together.

3 cups steamed small brussels
sprouts, cooled
2 cups chopped apples
2 cups chopped chestnuts
1/2 cup Tofu Mayonnaise
(p. 158) or Nut Milk
Mayonnaise (p. 151)

Curried Potato Salad

*1 recipe Curried Potatoes
    (p. 57), cooled
1 green pepper, chopped
1/2 cup chopped celery
1/2 cup yogurt*

Fold together all ingredients and let stand for at least 4 hours.

Green Bean and Feta Salad

*fresh whole green beans
feta cheese
vinaigrette*

1. Snap ends off of green beans and steam until emerald green. Drain.

2. Place them in a bowl and pour Vinaigrette (p. 90) over them. When cool, crumble feta cheese on.

3. Toss and chill at least 1 hour, better overnight.

Guacamole Salad

Fold all ingredients together and chill. Can be slightly mashed and eaten on toasted tortilla chips.

2 large avocados, cubed
2 large tomatoes, cubed
2 Tablespoons fresh lemon juice
1 teaspoon fresh chopped parsley
pinch chili powder
salt and pepper to taste

Linguini Salad

Fold all together. Adjust seasonings to taste.

1/4 pound linguini, broken into thirds and cooked
20 black olives, chopped coarsely
1/2 recipe of Mama Papa's Peppers (p. 80)
1 teaspoon fresh basil, snipped
4 tomatoes, chopped fine
salt to taste
olive oil to taste

Mama Papa's Peppers

Mrs. Papa was my sister's Italian grandmother-in-law. She made these for all their family gatherings. These are good alone or in a salad.

4 red peppers
1/4 cup olive oil
3/4 teaspoon salt

1. **Wash peppers. Remove stem and seed core.**

2. **Roast peppers in oven at 400° for 25 minutes, turning once.**

3. **Peel off skins and cut into long strips.**

4. **Mix with salt and oil and marinate overnight.**

Marinated Vegetables

Try:
    beets
    green beans
    wax beans
    carrots
    potatoes
    broccoli
    cauliflower

1. Steam vegetables until tender, though still firm. Green ones should be brilliant green.

2. Marinate in a Vinaigrette (p. 90) or Herb Vinegar (p. 89) at least 24 hours. Salt to taste if desired.

Pastafazool

Stir all together and let marinate in refrigerator overnight.

1 cup cooked kidney beans
3 cups spiral noodles, cooked
1/4 cup olive oil
3 Tablespoons cider vinegar

Potato and Miscellaneous Salad

I like crunchy things in my salad. If the refrigerator doesn't yield all of the above ingredients, I have also added 1/2 - 1 cup cooked drained beans or chickpeas, raw green beans or peas, 1/2 cup sunflower seeds (toasted) or bean sprouts. Potato salad and macaroni salad are good bases to experiment with.

6 potatoes, boiled and cubed

10 black or green olives

1/4 cup chopped pickles
  (any kind you like)

3 stalks chopped celery

1/3 cup chopped sweet pepper

1 Tablespoon salt
  (less if pickles are salty or if
  you use green olives)

2 teaspoons vinegar

1 1/2 cups yogurt or sour
  cream or mixture of both

Mix all ingredients and let sit at least 3 hours to blend flavors.

Variation:
Replace 1/2 cup of the yogurt/sour cream with 1/2 cup French Dressing (p. 88). Marinate overnight.

Salad in a Vegetable Cup

1. **Mix up the marinade of spices, oil, and vinegar.**

2. **Mix with grated cheeses and set aside for 15 minutes while preparing vegetable cups.**

3. **Cut off the tops of vegetables and scoop out the seed cavity. Tops may be replaced for travel.**

4. **Pack in cheese mixture and top with a few croutons.**

Variations:
Sweet red pepper - stuff with potato salad or other fillings.

Tomato - try Hummus (p. 41) or Linguini Salad (p. 79) (without the tomato in it) for filling.

4 bell peppers or 4 tomatoes
1/3 cup olive oil
2 Tablespoons cider vinegar
1 cup grated swiss cheese
1 cup grated mild cheddar
salt and pepper to taste
1 Tablespoon chopped fresh
    herb (try dill or marjoram
    or chive or basil)

Soy Tomato Aspic

My grandmother used to make this often. I've replaced the gelatin she used (non-vegetarian) with agar, which works just as well. Stays solid at room temperature. Good with Tofu Mayonnaise (p. 158).

1/2 teaspoon chopped fresh
    basil or dill
1/2 teaspoon chopped fresh
    parsley
1/2 pound tofu
    (kneaded until smoothly
    crumbled)
4 Tablespoons finely minced
    peppers
1/2 Tablespoon granulated
    agar
1 cup tomato juice (or V8)
1/4 teaspoon lemon juice
1 Tablespoon tamari

1. **Mix herbs, tofu and peppers together; set aside.**

2. **Combine liquids and agar in a saucepan and allow to sit for a few minutes.**

3. **Bring it to a boil, stirring constantly. Continue stirring and boil for 3 minutes.**

4. **Cool, stir in herb/tofu mix, pour into a mold and refrigerate until set.**

Tabouli

Mix all ingredients together; marinate overnight.

3 cups cooked bulgur
3/4 cup Italian dressing
1/3 cup chopped celery
1/3 cup chopped green or red
  bell pepper

Three to Five Bean Salad

1. **Pour marinade over beans.**

2. **Fold together gently and refrigerate 24 hours.**

1 cup cooked chickpeas
1 cup cooked green beans
  (cut 1 inch long)
1 cup cooked kidney beans
  (and/or wax and lima
  beans)

Marinade
Mix:
  1 part water
  2 parts vinegar
  2 parts oil
  1 part honey

Add:
  1 Tablespoon fresh
  chopped marjoram and 1
  teaspoon salt for each cup
  of liquid.

Turtle in the Mud Salad

This recipe started out as a joke which was enjoyed and became a regular. This doesn't look like a travelling salad, but the kids like to bring the components to school to assemble before their friends.

Turtle:

1/2 teaspoon granulated
    agar
2 Tablespoons lemon juice
1/2 cup water
1/2 cup finely chopped
    spinach
2 Tablespoons finely
    chopped dill
1/2 teaspoon salt
1 cup pureed cooked lima
    beans
1/4 cup cashew halves
3 olives cut into O's (to
    decorate the turtle's back)

The Turtle:

1. **Mix the water and agar together and let sit 2 minutes.**

2. **Bring to a boil and boil for 2 - 2 1/2 minutes, stirring. Cool.**

3. **Stir in lemon juice, lima bean puree, spinach and dill.**

4. **Refrigerate until set (about 2 hours).**

5. **Using a shallow-bowled tablespoon, scoop out oval shapes to be the turtle shell. These stay solid even at room temperature, but they water a bit overnight (just drain it off).**

Mud:

1/2 cup mayonnaise
    [or Tofu Mayonnaise
    (p. 158)]
1 Tablespoon miso

The Mud:

1. **Mash the miso with a fork until softened.**

2. **Add the Tofu Mayonnaise a little at a time.**

Set the Turtle into the Mud. Give him a head, tail, and feet of cashews and decorate his back with olive O's.

Vinegared Beets

I mix these with some cottage cheese and eat the pink stuff on lettuce for a quick summer lunch.

1. Steam or pressure cook beets.

2. Cut in slices or small cubes.

3. Marinate in beet-cooking water and vinegar (ratio of one to one) overnight.

beets
water
cider vinegar

Waldorf Salad

Stir all ingredients together.

1/2 cup raisins
1/2 cup celery, chopped
1/2 cup walnuts, chopped
1 cup apples, chopped
1 cup Nut Milk Mayonnaise
(p. 151)

DRESSINGS

Bleu Cheese Dressing

1 cup cottage cheese
1/4 cup yogurt
3 Tablespoons bleu cheese
pinch salt

Whiz ingredients in blender briefly.

Creamy Cucumber Dressing

1 peeled and finely chopped
   cucumber
1 cup yogurt
pinch salt
3 Tablespoons fresh minced
   dill

Stir all ingredients together.

French Dressing

2 Tablespoons honey
4 Tablespoons cider vinegar
1 teaspoon paprika
1 teaspoon salt
1/2 cup oil
1/4 cup yogurt
6 ounces cream cheese

1. **Melt cream cheese on low heat.**

2. **Remove from heat and whisk in all other ingredients.**

Herb Cheese Dressing

Process all ingredients together in a blender.

1/2 cup chopped fresh herbs
  (try: parsley, thyme, dill,
   basil or 1/4 cup tarragon)
1 cup cottage cheese
1 cup yogurt
pinch or two of salt

Herb Vinegars

A quick procedure is as follows:

1. **Put a few tablespoonsful of chopped herb in a jar.**

2. **Bring vinegar to a boil and pour over the herb.**

3. **Let sit overnight.**

4. **Strain out the herb and discard.**

5. **Pour vinegar into a bottle and place a sprig of whole herb in it. Set in dark place.**

A slower method is to place herbs and unheated vinegar in a sunny window for two weeks, shaking daily. Note: purple basil makes pink vinegar.

1 cup Tofu Mayonnaise
(p. 158)
1/4 cup ketchup
2 Tablespoons relish
1 teaspoon vinegar
1 teaspoon paprika
pinch salt
pinch wasabi powder

1/4 cup cider vinegar or
juice of 1/2 lemon
(optional)
3 Tablespoons tamari
1/2 cup olive oil
1/4 teaspoon chopped fresh
thyme
1/4 teaspoon chopped fresh
basil (if it isn't already in
the salad)
1/4 teaspoon chopped fresh
marjoram

3 Tablespoons cider vinegar
1 large ripe red tomato
3/4 teaspoon mustard
1 1/2 teaspoons fresh minced
thyme
tiny pinch freshly grated
black pepper

Russian Dressing

Stir all together.

Sumitra's House Dressing

Stir all ingredients together.

Vinaigrette

Whiz all ingredients together in a blender.

Chapter 5

Main Dishes

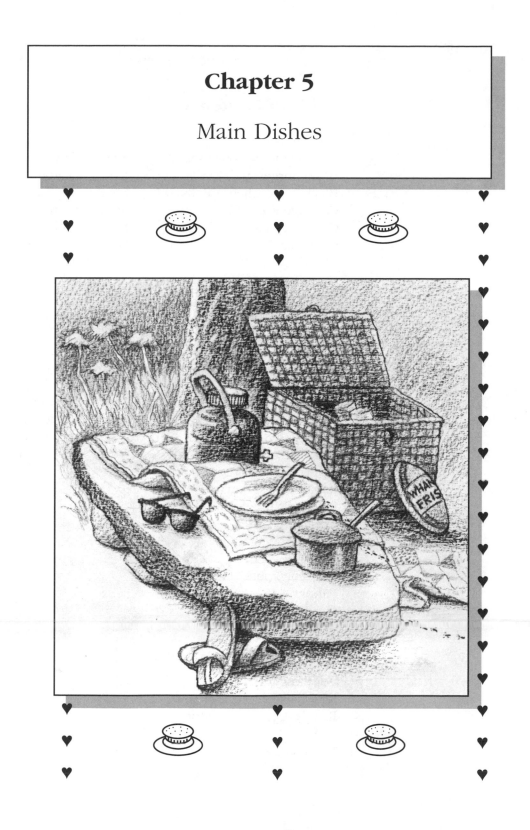

Table of Contents

CHAPTER FIVE: MAIN DISHES

Most of the following recipes are foods I usually make for dinner. Leftovers are for lunch. Sometimes a dinner is so well-liked that I have to double the portions so I can make lunches the next day (it's a policy at our house that I only cook once a day).

All of the foods in this section will hold their own shapes and are good hot or cold.

Asparagus in a Cast

bread
Tofu Mayonnaise
   (p. 158)
cooked asparagus
butter [or margarine]

1. Cut all the crusts off a slice of bread (save these for Burger mix—p. 96).

2. Flatten bread with a rolling pin and spread with mayonnaise.

3. Place asparagus on bread with 1/4 - 1/2 inch sticking out each end and roll asparagus up.

4. Brush with butter and bake seam side down for about 15 minutes at 375°, until lightly crusty.

Baked Stuffed Tomatoes

I like these cold with a squeeze of lemon on them.

1. **Cut tomatoes in half and scoop out insides.**

2. **Place chopped tomato insides and other ingredients in a skillet. On medium heat, stir together until all wilt and the butter melts.**

3. **Stuff into the tomato shells and bake at 350° for 20 - 30 minutes. Eat hot or cold.**

2 large tomatoes
2 Tablespoons butter
  [or margarine]
1 cup bread crumbs
pinch black pepper
pinch salt
1 Tablespoon minced fresh
  parsley
1/4 teaspoon thyme
1/4 teaspoon marjoram
2 Tablespoons parmesan
  cheese

Basic Burger

Burgers can be seasoned as you like. Nuts and seeds can be increased or left out. You can process any beans or leftover bean soup, and any grains, including leftover breakfast hot cereal. You can practically empty the refrigerator, just like with minestrone soup.

2 cups mashed beans
(soy, lentils, adzuki, or
others)
1/2 cup stock or water
(if the beans are a bit dry)
1 cup cooked grain
(rice, millet, bulgur, etc.)
1 cup toasted chopped nuts
or seeds
2 Tablespoons nutritional
yeast
1/4 cup tamari
1/4 teaspoon oregano
1/4 teaspoon thyme
salt and pepper to taste
1/2 cup raw shredded carrots
or finely chopped leftover
vegetables
2 cups or more oats
(bread crumbs can also be
used)

1. **Mash beans (puree).**

2. **Stir in remaining ingredients.**

3. **Add oats or bread crumbs as needed to stiffen dough.**

4. **Form into patties and fry on medium hot skillet in oil, both sides, or bake at 350° for 1/2 hour.**

Black Olive Cheese Balls

Combine all the ingredients and shape into balls. The size depends on appetite or how many you're serving.

2 Tablespoons tamari

1 teaspoon mustard powder

1/4 teaspoon ginger powder

pinch wasabi powder

1/4 cup fresh chopped herbs
(basil, thyme, chives,
parsley, or a combination)

1 pound mashed tofu

8 ounces cream cheese,
softened

1 1/2 cup grated mild
cheddar cheese

1 cup minced black olives

Cabbage Rolls

These are good dipped in a thermos cup of hot Tomato Cheese Soup (p. 53).

1. Drop cabbage into boiling water and simmer until the leaves are soft enough to be peeled off.

2. Separate and cool.

3. When cool enough to handle, place about 3 Tablespoons of filling in center of each leaf and roll up, folding in edges as you roll. Tie with a string or hold together with a toothpick for travel.

large head cabbage

filling:

2 cups cooked rice

1 cup cottage cheese

3 Tablespoons minced fresh
basil, dill, or thyme

Chestnut Chapeau

These are delicious cold with hot broth gravy.

1 cup chopped celery

1 cup chopped cabbage

1 Tablespoon oil

1 Tablespoon butter
   [or margarine

1 cup bread crumbs

1 Tablespoon nutritional
   yeast

1/4 teaspoon each: parsley,
   sage, rosemary, thyme,
   marjoram, ginger

a grating of fresh black
   pepper

3 cups cooked rice

1/4 cup chopped fresh
   parsley

4 Tablespoons tahini

salt to taste

2 cups chopped chestnuts

1. Saute celery and cabbage in oil and butter. When soft, stir in bread crumbs and saute briefly.

2. Remove from heat and stir in remaining ingredients.

3. Oil hands and shape mixture into little flat-bottomed balls of about a handful each. Add more bread crumbs as needed to give the desired consistency for shaping.

4. Bake at 300° for 1/2 hour.

Chickpea Souffle

1. Process soybeans, water, spices, and nuts in blender or food processor.

2. Slowly add chickpea flour and then oil.

3. Pour into a casserole and bake 15 minutes at 350°, then 1 1/2 hours at 300°.

4. Cool and eat with Cranberry Ketchup (p. 143).

2 cups soybeans that have
   been soaked overnight
2 1/2 cups water
1/2 teaspoon turmeric
2 Tablespoons nutritional
   yeast
1/2 teaspoon thyme
1/4 teaspoon hing
1/2 teaspoon sage
1/2 teaspoon parsley
2 teaspoons salt
2 Tablespoons pine nuts
   (optional)
1/3 cup chickpea flour
   (whiz chickpeas in a
   blender or food processor)
1/4 cup oil

1 cup chopped cabbage
1/2 green pepper, chopped
1/4 cup olive oil
1 cup tomato puree
1 Tablespoon chili powder
1 cup chopped Soy Scrapple
    (p. 127)
1 pound bread dough

Chili Fingers

1. **Saute cabbage and green pepper in olive oil.**

2. **Add tomato puree, chili powder, and Soy Scrapple. Simmer 10 minutes. (This makes a chili base)**

3. **Roll 1 pound bread dough into rectangles 1/8 inch thick.**

4. **Spread on chili mix about 1/4 inch thick.**

5. **Roll up and place on an oiled baking sheet.**

6. **Place in a cold oven, set temperature to 350°, and bake for 35 minutes or until golden.**

Variation:
If you haven't any Soy Scrapple in the freezer, use 1 cup steamed soy grits or steamed texturized vegetable protein, but increase the spicing and simmer for about 15 minutes.

Corn Fritters

We eat these with maple syrup, though they taste good dipped in Sweet and Sour Sauce (p. 157) or salsa.

1/4 pound tofu
1/4 cup milk
2/3 cup flour
1/2 teaspoon salt
1/2 teaspoon baking powder
1 cup corn

1. **Puree milk and tofu together.**

2. **Mix in remaining ingredients and stir in the corn.**

3. **Drop walnut sized pieces in hot oil and cook until golden. Drain on paper towels.**

Crusty Loaf

When ready to eat, slice loaf 1 inch thick at a slight slant to get parabolas. Fun for a picnic, or can be made in a crusty roll for individual lunches. Send along a sauce or mayonnaise.

1 loaf Italian bread
butter [or margarine]
filling:
   Sopnut (p. 43),
   Soy Scrapple (p. 127),
   Nut Loaf (p. 137),
   or ground Brown
     Gluten (p. 108)

1. **Cut off one end tip of an Italian loaf and scoop out the insides, leaving a 1/2 inch layer all around.**

2. **Butter the inside to keep bread from getting soggy, and pack the filling tightly into the bread cave.**

3. **Wrap and refrigerate a few hours, until set up.**

Crusty Potatoes

The kids like this dish cold with applesauce, ketchup, or Peach Chutney (p. 152) on top, or warm with creamed spinach poured over it. I like it with Cranberry Ketchup (p. 143) or spicy Tofu Mayonnaise (p. 158).

5 medium-sized red or white
  potatoes, peeled
a bowl of ice water
3 Tablespoons oil
2 Tablespoons butter
  [or margarine]
1/4 teaspoon pepper
1/2 teaspoon salt

1. Grate potatoes into ice water. Let sit 15 minutes. Drain and pat dry.

2. In a large fry pan, heat the butter and oil. Mix the potato with spices and pack into the fry pan.

3. Keep on low heat until golden on bottom, flip and fry the other side.

4. Cut into squares or slice like a pie.

Eggplant Fries

These go well with Tofu Tartar Sauce (p. 158) or with salsa.

1. Peel the eggplant and cut into strips 1/2 inch thick.

2. Mix remaining ingredients (except oil), letting ice cubes float in the mix.

3. Dip the eggplant strips into this mix and fry in hot oil. Drain on paper towels.

1 eggplant
1/2 cup unbleached flour
1/4 teaspoon baking powder
1/4 teaspoon salt
1/4 teaspoon paprika
2 Tablespoons grated
  parmesan cheese
1/2 cup water
2 ice cubes
oil

Eggplant Rolls

These taste fine cold, or you can box up the eggplant rolls and thermos up the hot tomato sauce.

1 eggplant, sliced 1/4 inch
   thick
1/4 cup olive oil
2 cups tomato sauce

filling:
1 cup ricotta cheese
3 Tablespoons parmesan
   cheese
2 Tablespoons freshly
   chopped basil or marjoram

1. Sprinkle each slice of eggplant with salt and let sit 1/2 hour.

2. Brush moisture and salt off and fry in olive oil, lightly on each side.

3. Spread each slice with filling, roll up, and tie with string or secure with tooth pick.

4. Pour tomato sauce over and bake at 350° for 1/2 hour.

Falafels

These are traditionally stuffed in pita bread, but my kids prefer me to send along a cocktail sword so that they can spear them and dip them in Cranberry Ketchup (p. 143) or Peach Chutney (p. 152).

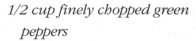

1. **Saute green pepper and cabbage in oil.**

2. **Combine these with remaining ingredients and with enough bread crumbs to hold it together.**

3. **Roll into balls the size of large marbles and drop-fry in hot oil or flatten slightly and bake about 15 minutes in a 300° oven.**

1/2 cup finely chopped green peppers
1 cup finely chopped cabbage
3 Tablespoons oil (olive oil is nice)
2 cups chickpea puree (see Soy Puree, p. 123)
1 Tablespoon parsley flakes
2 Tablespoons tahini
1 teaspoon cumin
1/4 teaspoon black pepper
1 - 1 1/2 cup bread crumbs

French Toast

1/4 cup cashew butter
   or almond butter
2/3 cup milk
bread

1. Blend nut butter and milk in a blender or food processor.

2. Soak bread quickly both sides in this mix and fry in butter or margarine.

3. Dust lightly with cinnamon or a grate of nutmeg. Cut into strips (the easier to dip with).

Variation:
Grind raw cashews or almonds in a blender or food processor to a fine meal. Slowly add milk until mixture thickens. Dip bread in and fry as above.

Ginger Tofu Steam Buns

These are good with spicy Tofu Mayonnaise (p. 158).

1. **Mix filling ingredients and set aside.**

2. **In a bowl, mix warm water, yeast, and honey. Let set for 5 minutes, until yeast blooms.**

3. **Stir in remaining ingredients and let rise 45 minutes.**

4. **Knead down and divide into ping pong size pieces.**

5. **Roll each out into a 3 inch circle and put a glob of filling in the center.**

6. **Gather all the edges up and pinch together. Set in a warm place, seam side down on a steaming rack for 15 minutes to rise.**

7. **Steam above boiling water for 15 minutes.**

Filling:
1 pound tofu, mashed
1 Tablespoon grated fresh
* ginger*
1 Tablespoon tamari
2 Tablespoons sesame seeds
pinch salt
1 teaspoon oil

Dough wrapper:
2 1/4 cups flour
1 teaspoon yeast
1 teaspoon honey
1 Tablespoon oil
1 cup warm water
1/2 teaspoon salt

Gluten

This is the protein part of the wheat. It is starchless and is a great meat substitute. However, if you don't digest wheat well, this isn't for you. Look for a brand of high-gluten white flour that is not bleached.

Note: the longer you knead and simmer the gluten, the tougher it will be. You can achieve a whole range of textures from soft dumpling to meat-like chewiness.

For brown gluten:
simmer in Brown Broth
(p. 64)

For yellow gluten:
simmer in Yellow Broth
(p. 64)

Quick Method:

1 cup gluten flour
1 cup water

1. Stir together gluten flour and water, adding more water if necessary, to achieve a thick dough.

2. Knead the dough to develop elasticity in the gluten and squeeze out excess water.

3. Break into small pieces (about 1 inch in diameter) and drop into a boiling broth (brown, yellow, vegetable or sea broth).

4. Simmer at least 1/2 hour.

Variation:
If you cannot get gluten flour, follow these steps.

6 cups wheat flour (whole wheat or unbleached white)

1. Mix together and knead wheat flour and water for about 20 minutes to develop the glutens.

1 1/2 cups cold water

2. Submerge the dough in a bowl of cold water for an hour.

a bowl of cold water

3. Start kneading dough under the water (gently at first). The water will turn white as the starch is released into it. Pour off this water and continue kneading under new water. Repeat this until the water clears. This, now, is the raw gluten. Follow directions starting with number 3 above.

Golden Tofu Nuggets

1. **Press and drain tofu.**

2. **Cut into 3/4 inch cubes.**

3. **In a plastic bag, mix nutritional yeast and corn-starch. Throw tofu cubes in and shake until all coated.**

4. **Drop nuggets into hot oil in a heavy skillet. Oil should be about up to their "waists" so when you flip them, they will be done on all sides.**

5. **Drain on paper towels. Salt and eat with Tofu Tartar Sauce (p. 158) or spicy Tofu Mayonnaise (p. 158).**

tofu
1 part nutritional yeast
1 part arrowroot or
  cornstarch
salt to taste
oil for frying

Honey Fried Tofu

1 pound tofu
2 Tablespoons honey
2 Tablespoons butter

1. Cut tofu into 1/2 inch cubes.

2. In a heavy skillet, melt butter, add honey, and stir in tofu.

3. Simmer and fry until golden. Salt to taste.

Italian Cereal Squares

I invented this when I was pregnant and I needed to eat within 10 minutes of rising or succumb to morning sickness. Sometimes, I send along a little extra parmesan to sprinkle on lunches.

1/2 cup chopped vegetables
    (black olives, chives, green
    peppers, sprouts, cabbage)
1 cup grated cheese
    (mozzarella and cheddar)
1 cup water
1/2 cup cream of wheat
    (uncooked)
1 cup seasoned tomato sauce
salt to taste

1. Chop vegetables, grate cheese, and bring water to a boil.

2. Stir cereal and vegetables into boiling water. Simmer 3 minutes.

3. Add tomato sauce when cooked to a slightly sticky consistency.

4. Quickly stir in cheese and pour into a square pan. When somewhat cooled, cut into squares.

Jeweled Yuba Logs

1. Cut off the tops of the pepper and tomato and scoop out the seeds and insides.

2. Cut into a continuous strip 1/4 - 1/2 inch wide. Cut to the same length as cucumber so that you have jullienne strips of all the vegetables, the length of yuba sheets.

3. Arrange cucumber pieces, pepper and tomato pieces in a bundle in the center of yuba sheets and roll all into a log shape.

4. Roll in wax paper and twist the ends. This can be cut into circles about 1 inch thick and served with a dollop of mayonnaise.

1 green pepper

1 ripe tomato

1 cucumber, cut into quarters lengthwise and then cut to the length of the yuba sheets

3 sheets reconstituted yuba (steam lightly 1 minute to soften)

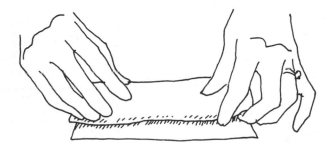

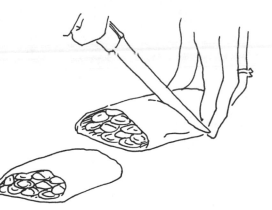

Kohlrabi Cups

4 kohlrabies
1 cup cabbage, finely
   chopped
1 Tablespoon butter
   [or margarine]
2 Tablespoons walnuts,
   processed in blender
1 cup Soy Scrapple (p. 127)
1/4 pound mashed tofu
1/2 cup sour cream

1. Peel the kohlrabi and steam until tender.

2. Scoop out the centers, leaving 1/2 inch thick walls.

3. Saute the cabbage in butter until it wilts.

4. Add the other ingredients, except walnuts. Stir in sour cream.

5. Fill the cups and top with the walnuts.

6. Bake at 400° in an oiled pan for 10 - 20 minutes, until all the flavors blend.

Madhuri Ricotta Quiche

1. **Mix the cheeses and spices; fold in spinach.**

2. **Spread into pie crust and bake at 350° for 30 minutes.**

9 inch pie crust
2 pounds ricotta cheese
1/4 cup grated parmesan
*   cheese*
1/4 cup grated romano
cheese
1/2 teaspoon oregano
1/4 teaspoon basil
1/4 teaspoon thyme
1/4 teaspoon salt
dash pepper
2 cups chopped fresh spinach

Oatey Pie

1. **Mix oats, spices and 1 cup cheese into soft butter.**

2. **Spread on pie crust and sprinkle top with remainder of cheese.**

3. **Bake at 425° for 15 - 20 minutes. Cut into wedges.**

9 inch pie crust
1 cup oats
1 1/2 cup grated sharp
*   cheddar cheese*
3 Tablespoons butter,
*   softened*
1 teaspoon paprika
pinch salt
1 teaspoon prepared mustard

1 cup grated sharp cheddar
    cheese
2/3 cup flour
1/2 stick butter or margarine
2 dozen small pitted black
    olives
1/4 teaspoon salt
1/4 teaspoon paprika

Olie en Croute

1. Soften butter and stir in cheese.

2. Add spices and flour.

3. Surround an olive with about 1 teaspoon of this dough and place it on a flat sheet. Continue until all the dough is used. (You can use little raw cauliflower florettes if you like)

4. Freeze the dough balls on the sheet. When frozen, repack in an airtight container. Whenever you want to use a few, thaw on a baking sheet for 1/2 hour or in the refrigerator overnight. Bake at 425° for about 15 minutes.

Pakora

1. **Mix dry ingredients first.**

2. **Stir in water, then ice cubes.**

3. **When the ice cubes start to melt, it is time to dip vegetables into the batter and deep fry until golden (the ice keeps the batter cold, which helps it to puff up when fried). Drain on paper towels.**

1 cup chickpea flour
2 Tablespoons arrowroot
    or cornstarch
1 teaspoon salt
1/2 cup water
3 ice cubes

vegetables for pakora:
pepper rings
cauliflower florettes
broccoli florettes
eggplant chunks
squash cut into thin
    rectangles

Pan Fried Tofu

1. **Heat oil in a skillet.**

2. **Slice tofu in slabs and drain.**

3. **Fry in oil on each side until golden brown or as crispy as you like. While frying, sprinkle salt or tamari on each piece.**

tofu or defrosted frozen tofu
    (squeeze the water out)
oil
salt or tamari

Polenta

Eat this with hot Spicy Mexican Vegetables (p. 68), or Refried Bean Spread (p. 42) and a dollop of sour cream or yogurt.

5 cups water
1 teaspoon salt
1 cup cornmeal

1. Combine ingredients in a saucepan and stir over medium heat.

2. Whisk out lumps. When it thickens, pour into an oiled pan or dish. When it is cool, slide it out and slice.

Cheese Polenta:
Just before pouring into oiled pan or dish, stir in 1/2 cup grated mild cheddar and 1/2 cup grated parmesan cheeses.

Spicy Polenta:
Add 2 teaspoons cumin powder and 1/4 teaspoon cayenne while cooking polenta.

Potato Balls

1. **Mix all ingredients together.**

2. **Roll into 1 inch balls and fry in hot oil until golden.**

2 cups mashed potatoes
1 1/2 cup flour
1 teaspoon curry powder
    (optional)
salt to taste

Potato Griddlecakes

These cakes are good hot or cold. Try them with thermos-held hot Cream of Any Vegetable Soup (p. 55) spooned over them, or spread with apple butter.

1. **Process water, cornstarch and tofu in blender or food processor.**

2. **Pour into a bowl and add the yeast. Let dissolve and bloom to top.**

3. **Add flour, potato and salt. Beat well with wooden spoon.**

4. **Let rise for 1/2 hour. Beat again and pour little cakes onto a medium temperature, well greased griddle. Flip when browned and cook other side.**

1 cup hot water
1/4 pound tofu
1 teaspoon cornstarch
1 Tablespoon baking yeast
1 cup grated potatoes
3/4 cup whole wheat flour
1 teaspoon salt

Pot Pies

I usually make a large Pot Pie in a dutch oven, and it ends up in thermoses, but individual ones can go to the office to be heated in an oven or microwave. Alternatively, you can use puff pastry or pie crust, make individual turnovers, or simply send along one of the Nests (p. 20-21) to fill.

For a quick method, put cubed tofu in a casserole and add a bag of frozen mixed vegetables. Pour a white sauce over all and cover with a few filo leaves flecked with butter. Bake until bubbly and crusty.

Filling:

1 pound tofu

3 medium potatoes

1 carrot

2 cups peas

1 cup chopped turnip

1 cup water

3 Tablespoons butter
   [or margarine]

2 Tablespoons flour

2 cups milk

1/4 cup sour cream

salt and pepper to taste

1. **Simmer vegetables and tofu in water until tender. Set aside.**

2. **In another saucepan, melt butter, stir in flour, and slowly add milk while stirring. Simmer, stirring, until thick.**

3. **Add white sauce to tofu and vegetables. Fold in sour cream.**

4. **Pour into a casserole dish.**

5. **Stir crust ingredients together.**

6. **Scoop out large spoonsful of dumpling dough and pat to flatten slightly.**

7. **Drop each biscuit on top of filling. The dumplings should cover the top of filling with their edges touching.**

8. **Bake until browned and bubbly.**

Dumpling Crust:

1/2 cup flour

1/2 cup water

1/4 cup sour cream

1/2 teaspoon baking soda

1/4 teaspoon salt

1 Tablespoon honey

Rice Balls

I like these with spicy Tofu Mayonnaise (p. 158) for a dipping sauce.

1. While rice is still warm, mix in tahini and cornstarch.

2. Mix up the other ingredients to make a stuffing.

3. Put about 1/3 cup of the rice mix in your cupped hand, leaving a little hollow in the center.

4. Put about 2 Tablespoons of the stuffing in the hollow, sprinkle more rice mix over the top and pack with two hands. No stuffing should show. Re-sprinkle areas where it peeks through and pack well again.

5. Heat oil and fry until golden.

5 cups cooked rice

1 teaspoon tahini

1 Tablespoon cornstarch

1 cup shredded cheese

1/2 cup mashed tofu

1/4 cup tomato sauce

1/2 teaspoon salt

3/4 cup cooked chickpeas or green peas

1/3 cup finely chopped almonds

Rice Nuggets Monadnock

These nuggets climbed Mt. Monadnock in New Hampshire (the second most climbed mountain in the world).

2 cups cooked brown rice

1/2 cup pureed kidney beans

2 cups finely chopped kale

1 cup mashed cooked
   pumpkin or squash

1/2 cup walnut meal

1 cup whole wheat bread
   crumbs

1. **Lightly steam the kale until wilted.**

2. **Add 1/2 of the bread crumbs and remaining ingredients.**

3. **Roll into 1 inch balls and roll in bread crumbs.**

4. **Bake at 350° for 30 minutes, or until golden brown.**

Rumpledethumps

1. Pour half of the butter in the bottom of a shallow square baking dish.

2. Sprinkle the bread crumbs on the butter.

3. Pack the mashed potatoes on top of this, 3/4 - 1 inch thick.

4. Saute the cabbage and cashews in the remaining butter, mix in the cut corn, and set aside.

5. Spread cottage cheese (ricotta cheese or tofu) on top of the potatoes. Sprinkle on the herbs.

6. Spread on the cabbage and nuts and top with grated cheese.

7. Bake at 350° for 20 minutes. Cool and cut into squares.

4 Tablespoons melted butter [or margarine]

1 cup bread crumbs

3 cups mashed potatoes (you can use leftovers)

3 cups finely chopped cabbage

1/2 cup chopped cashews

1 cup cottage cheese, ricotta cheese [or mashed tofu]

2 cups cut corn

1/4 cup fresh chopped herbs (parsely or dill weed)

1 cup grated mild cheddar cheese

1/4 teaspoon salt

Savory Vegetable Cake

Thermos-held hot Vegetable Broth Gravy (p. 58) is nice poured over this when the cake is cold.

1. **Lightly saute vegetables in butter in an oven-proof skillet until they turn bright. Add the beans and olives, and set aside.**

2. **In a bowl, mix up a batter of the remaining ingredients.**

3. **Pour the batter over the vegetables in the skillet and bake at 300° for 45 minutes.**

4. **Flip it over onto a plate and cut into wedges. Eat hot or cold.**

3 Tablespoons butter
  [or margarine]
1/2 cup grated carrots
1 cup cut corn
1/2 cup chopped broccoli
1/2 cup cooked kidney
  beans
1/2 cup chopped black
  olives
1 1/2 teaspoons baking
  powder
3/4 cup milk [or soy or nut
  milk]
1/4 cup yogurt
2 Tablespoons tahini
1 teaspoon parsley, chopped
pinch black pepper
1 Tablespoon sunflower
  seeds
1/2 cup grated parmesan
1 1/2 cups whole wheat
  flour
1/4 cup nutritional yeast
1 teaspoon salt

Scumps

When packaging, I box these with noodles and later pour a thermos-held hot gravy (p. 58) over all.

Form this mix into ping pong sized balls and fry in hot oil or bake at 350° for 20 minutes.

1 cup cooked grain (millet, bulgur, brown rice, etc.)

1 cup soy grits (cooked) or soy puree (puree: soak soybeans for 24 hours and add to enough water to puree in blender)

1/2 cup or more bread crumbs to hold all together

1/4 cup grated cheese (optional)

1 Tablespoon tahini

3 Tablespoons tamari

1/4 teaspoon salt

pinch pepper

1 Tablespoon brewers yeast (optional)

Skillet Potatoes

1 teaspoon oil

1/3 cup shredded cabbage

3 cups cold cooked potatoes,
    cubed in 1/4 inch pieces

1/4 teaspoon salt

pinch pepper

3 Tablespoons flour

1/4 cup milk [or soy or nut
    milk]

2 - 4 Tablespoons oil for
    frying

1. Saute cabbage in 1 teaspoon oil until soft.

2. Mix cabbage and other ingredients in a bowl except the 2 - 4 Tablespoons oil.

3. Heat a skillet, coat the bottom with oil and pack in the potato mix. Cook on low heat until golden, flip and cook other side. Cut into wedges like a pie.

Sombreros

Send along a small container of sour cream or yogurt for topping.

1. **Saute cabbage, pepper, and celery in oil until cabbage is soft.**

2. **Mix the thyme, cayenne, hing, salt, beans, corn, and tomato puree with 2 teaspoons of the cumin. Add to the vegetable mixture. Simmer until it thickens, about 15 minutes. Set aside.**

3. **To make polenta, mix water with cornmeal, 1/2 teaspoon cumin, salt, and a dash of cayenne. Cook until thick as pudding, stirring constantly. Add olives.**

4. **Spread half the polenta (while still warm) in a greased baking dish. Spread the bean/vegetable mix on it. Sprinkle with grated cheese. Spread on remaining polenta.**

5. **Bake in a 350° oven for about 30 minutes. Cool 15 minutes and cut into squares.**

2 cups shredded cabbage

1 green pepper, cored and chopped

1 cup chopped celery

3 Tablespoons oil

2 1/2 teaspoons cumin

1/4 teaspoon thyme

1/4 teaspoon cayenne

1/4 teaspoon hing

1 teaspoon salt

3 cups cooked pinto beans

2 cups corn

1/2 cup tomato puree

1/2 cup grated jack or cheddar cheese

polenta:

3 cups water

1 3/4 cups cornmeal

1/2 teaspoon cumin

pinch salt

dash cayenne

1 cup finely chopped olives

Somewhat Knishes

These are filled with your choice of fillings from Chapter Two.

1/2 cup mashed potatoes
1 1/2 cups whole wheat
    pastry flour
1/2 teaspoon salt
1/2 teaspoon baking powder
2 Tablespoons oil
1/3 cup water

1. Knead all ingredients together and let rest for 30 minutes.

2. Roll out very thin and cut into rectangles.

3. Place some filling in the center, fold corners in and seal.

4. Place seamed side down on an oiled baking pan. Brush with butter and bake at 350° for 30 minutes.

Soy Scrapple

Soy Scrapple is a high protein meat substitute which can be eaten without frying as a filling or in a sandwich with tartar sauce. Fried, it makes a great main dish, breakfast "soysage," taco filling or burger. This recipe fills approximately 5 pint jars. To store, remove from jars, pack in plastic bags, and freeze.

1. Mix all ingredients together.

2. Pack into greased cans or greased wide-mouth straight sided canning jars, 3/4 full. Cover with foil and hold it in place with rubber bands.

3. Place jars or cans on a trivet waist-deep in water in a covered pot and steam for 1 1/2 hours (a little longer if using large cans). When cool, slice and fry.

5 cups soy puree (soak 2 1/2 cups soybeans in 2 1/2 cups water overnight and puree in blender or food processor with enough liquid to do so; should have a thick, mealy consistency)

1 cup cornmeal

1 1/2 cups nutritional yeast

1 Tablespoon parsley

3 Tablespoons sage

1 Tablespoon fennel seed

3 Tablespoons thyme

1 Tablespoon salt

1 Tablespoon allspice

1 Tablespoon molasses

2 Tablespoons honey

3 Tablespoons prepared mustard

2 teaspoons pepper

1/3 cup tamari

1 cup oil

2 teaspoons hickory flavor (optional)

Soy Souffle

This tastes good eaten topped with spicy Tofu Mayonnaise (p. 158) and mustard.

2 cups tomatoes
1/4 teaspoon chopped parsley
1/4 teaspoon basil
1/4 teaspoon hing
1/4 teaspoon salt
few drops sesame oil
1 cup soy flour
1/2 cup water
1/4 cup parmesan cheese
1/4 cup oil

1. **Process tomatoes, water and spices in blender or food processor.**

2. **Slowly add soy flour and then oil while blending.**

3. **Pour into a flat baking dish about 1 inch thick and bake at 450° for 15 minutes.**

4. **Lower the heat to 250° and bake another 45 minutes. Cover and cool. Slice cold.**

Spiced Stuffed Peppers

1. **Mix together all but tomato sauce and peppers.**

2. **Cut off tops of peppers and scoop out seeds.**

3. **Stuff with mixture.**

4. **Pour thin tomato sauce over all, cover and bake 45 minutes at 350°.**

1 cup Soy Scrapple (p. 127)
1/2 cup light cream
1 1/4 pounds tofu
1 teaspoon fresh basil, chopped
1 1/2 teaspoons salt
1/2 cup chopped almonds
2-3 cups thin tomato sauce
6 green bell peppers

Spring Rolls

Spiced tofu is sometimes available in oriental food stores. I usually don't have it, so I simmer firm tofu, diced small, in tamari and ginger until crusty, about 10-15 minutes.

12 spring roll wrappers
   (some wrappers are made
   with eggs, others not)
2 cups bean sprouts
3/4 cup spiced tofu
3 cups shredded cabbage
2 cups shredded spinach
1 cup shredded carrots or
   other vegetables (optional)

1. Chop or shred sprouts, tofu, cabbage, spinach, and carrots fine.

2. Place about 3 Tablespoons of this filling in the center of a square wrapper. Fold the bottom corner up over the filling and tuck in the ends. Then roll up. When you reach the last corner, dip your fingers in water and rub the flap to seal it (rubbing a bit of cornstarch on the corner will help).

3. Place flap side down in a pan of hot oil. When golden, roll over until all sides are golden.

4. Drain on paper towel. Send along a cup of Sweet and Sour Sauce (p. 157) for dipping.

A.

B.

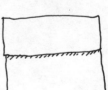

C.

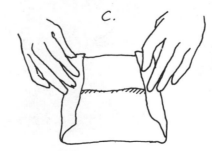

D.

Stuffed Tofu

1. Briefly steam spinach until it wilts. Stir in cheese and cover. Set aside.

1 pound tofu
4 Tablespoons oil
3 cups chopped spinach
1 cup grated cheddar cheese
salt to taste

2. Heat oil in a skillet. Slice a block of firm tofu into 1 inch thick slabs; press gently to drain.

3. Fry in hot oil.

4. Cut each square of tofu across diagonally and cut out the middle of each triangle to make a pocket, leaving a 1/4 inch thick wall.

5. Gently press spinach-cheese stuffing inside. Salt and paprika surface of tofu.

A.

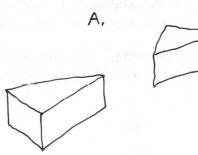

B.

Vegetarian Sushi (Nori Rolls)

1/2 pound tofu, sliced
  1/4 - 1/2 inch thick
oil to fry tofu
1 Tablespoon honey
1 Tablespoon vinegar
pinch salt
1 peeled cucumber
1 carrot
6 sheets of nori seaweed
1 umoboshi plum, pureed to
  a paste
3 cups brown rice, cooked

1. **Fry tofu slices in oil. Set aside.**

2. **Simmer the honey, vinegar, and salt gently in a heavy pot until all the liquid is gone.**

3. **Slice the tofu, the peeled cucumber, and the carrot into "match sticks."**

4. **Place a sheet of nori on a dry cutting board and spread about 1/2 cup of the brown rice on a sheet, leaving a 1/2 inch margin on the far edge.**

5. **Place a little bundle of "match sticks" in the center and sprinkle it lightly with bits of umoboshi paste.**

6. **Roll up going towards the seaweed margin. Wet the margin and seal. Wrap in waxed paper and twist ends.**

7. **Repeat for each roll. When eating, open one end and peel wax paper down as you eat. Eat with spicy Tofu Mayonnaise (p. 158).**

Tempura

1. **Mix dry ingredients.**

2. **Stir in water, then ice cubes.**

3. **Heat oil for deep frying (for successful deep frying the oil must be hot and the batter cold).**

4. **Dip each vegetable in the batter, place it in the oil and retrieve it with a slotted spoon when it is golden.**

5. **Drain on paper towels.**

1 cup whole wheat flour
1/2 cup gluten flour
1/2 teaspoon salt
1 cup cold water
2-3 ice cubes

vegetables for tempura:
pepper rings
cauliflower florettes
broccoli florettes
eggplant chunks
squash cut into thin
*   rectangles*

Tofu Flory

puff pastry
9 pieces 1 x 1/2 x 2 inch
   Brown Gluten (p. 108)
1 cup gravy
1 teaspoon chopped parsley
1/3 pound mashed tofu

1. **Thaw a piece of puff pastry. Unfold on floured board and cut into 9 squares. Roll out each square.**

2. **Make a gravy by adding 1 Tablespoon whole wheat flour to 1 cup brown broth from the gluten. Stir over low heat until thickened.**

3. **Add parsley and tofu to the gravy.**

4. **Place 1 Tablespoon of this mix and 1 piece Brown Gluten on the puff pastry and fold the pastry diagonally to make triangles.**

5. **Crimp the edges with a fork and bake at 375° for about 20 minutes.**

Tofu Quiche

Great hot or cold.

1. Melt butter in a saucepan,

2. Add flour, then milk, paprika, and salt. On low heat, make a thick cream sauce.

3. Add grated cheese, mashed tofu, and spinach.

4. Stir together and fill pie crust. Bake at 350° for 30 minutes.

4 Tablespoons butter [or margarine]

3 Tablespoons whole wheat flour

1/4 cup milk

1/4 teaspoon paprika

1/2 teaspoon salt

6 ounces grated sharp cheddar cheese

1 1/2 pounds tofu, mashed

1 pound spinach, chopped and steamed until wilted or defrost and drain a package of frozen spinach

9 inch pie crust

Tofu Telephones

The children named these one night while playing with their dinners. Whenever I put them in their lunchboxes, they promise to give me a call at noon.

3/4 pound tofu, firm and
  well drained
1 cup cooked brown rice
1 Tablespoon tahini
1 teaspoon soy sauce
1/4 teaspoon sesame oil
1/2 teaspoon salt

1. Mix all ingredients together.

2. Shape into crescents, roll in bread crumbs or nut meal and bake at 350° for 20 minutes. They can also be fried. Good with a dipping sauce or gravy.

Vermont Nut Loaf

This is really delicious and obviously has a lot of protein. I'm not quite sure of its origins; I call my friend Cirasmita in Vermont whenever I need the recipe, just as she calls me every summer to get the recipe for dill pickles. For some reason we have done this for years.

1. **Saute vegetables in butter.**

2. **Add all other ingredients and mix.**

3. **Pack into oiled loaf pans and bake at 375° for 75 minutes.**

3 Tablespoons butter
   [or margarine]
1 cup chopped celery
1 cup chopped cabbage
1/2 cup sesame seed meal
   (grind seeds in blender or
   food processor)
1/2 cup sunflower seed meal
1 pound cottage cheese [or 2
   cups Soy Curds—p. 161]
3 Tablespoons powdered soy
   milk
1/2 cup cooked brown rice
   (leftovers)
1/2 teaspoon chopped parsley
   and thyme
1/2 cup oats or bread crumbs
1 cup chopped toasted
   almonds
1 cup chopped pecans or
   walnuts
1 cup chopped toasted
   cashews
1/4 - 1/2 cup water

Welsh Rarebit

I'm not sure of the authenticity of this recipe, but it's what my family has always called Welsh Rarebit.

3 Tablespoons butter [or margarine]

3 Tablespoons whole wheat flour

1 cup milk

1 cup grated sharp cheddar cheese

1/2 teaspoon mustard powder

1. Melt butter, add flour and brown lightly.

2. Over low heat, slowly add milk, stirring continuously.

3. When the sauce thickens, add cheese and mustard. Heat until the cheese melts.

4. Serve over toast or biscuits.

Yeasty Vegetarian Omelettes

Package a bit of chutney to eat along with these.

1 cup nutritional yeast flakes

1 cup white flour

1 teaspoon curry powder

1/2 teaspoon salt

1 1/2 cups water

1/2 pound tofu

1/4 cup chopped cabbage

1 Tablespoon sunflower seeds

1/4 cup chopped celery

1/4 cup grated cheddar cheese

1/4 cup grated carrot

1. Mix dry ingredients.

2. Process tofu and water and add to dry ingredients.

3. Fold in seeds and chopped and grated items.

4. Cook on an oiled skillet at medium temperature until golden on both sides. (I pour these out onto a skillet in about 3 inch rounds for ease of turning.)

Chapter 6

Condiments, Sauces & Snacks

Table of Contents

CHAPTER SIX: CONDIMENTS, SAUCES & SNACKS

Whenever I think of packing condiments and dips for lunch, I think of a little badger named Francis from Hoban's book *Bread and Jam for Francis.* She brings her lunch to school (after being cured of a desire for only bread and jam meals) and lays a paper doily on her desk, sets a tiny vase of violets in the middle of it, and arranges around it her lunch of *"a thermos bottle with cream of tomato soup, a lobster salad sandwich on thin slices of white bread, celery, carrot sticks, and black olives, and a little cardboard shaker of salt for the celery. And two plums and a tiny basket of cherries. And vanilla pudding with chocolate sprinkles and a spoon to eat it with."*

My family loves dipping, dunking, sprinkling, pouring, and generally playing with their food, so these recipes are well-liked.

1 cup cabbage, chopped

4 Tablespoons oil

1/2 teaspoon hing

2 cups tomato puree

1/2 cup honey

1/2 cup molasses

1 Tablespoon salt

1 Tablespoon dried mustard

pinch cayenne pepper

1/2 teaspoon allspice

1/2 cup cider vinegar

1/8 cup soy sauce (tamari)

Barbecue Sauce

1. Saute cabbage in oil until translucent.

2. Add all but vinegar and tamari.

3. Simmer 45 minutes then add soy sauce (tamari) and vinegar. Simmer 10 minutes more. Freeze or store in refrigerator up to three weeks.

Cranberry Ketchup

This is good with curried foods, nut loaves, and fried foods.

1. Simmer cranberries in water until they pop and soften.

2. Whiz in blender or food processor and add remaining ingredients. Simmer 20 minutes. Cool. Freeze or store in refrigerator up to three weeks.

1 pound cranberries

1 cup water

1/2 cup molasses

1/2 cup honey

1/2 cup vinegar

1/4 teaspoon allspice

1/4 teaspoon cloves

1 teaspoon salt

Delectable Yam Sauce

Try this poured on cold steamed broccoli and cauliflower, or mix it with leftover stir-fry vegetables and pack it hot into a thermos. Very high in A and B vitamins and protein.

1/2 cup peanut butter

1- 3 cups water

2 cups mashed cooked yams
   or sweet potatoes

3/4 cup nutritional yeast

2 Tablespoons tamari

1/2 teaspoon salt

1 teaspoon paprika

1 teaspoon tumeric

1 1/2 teaspoons cumin

1. Melt peanut butter in 1 cup of the water.

2. Add remaining ingredients with remaining water to desired thickness. Simmer 10 minutes. Will keep in refrigerator for a week.

D.V.'s Green Tomato Relish

My friend D.V.'s family eats a lot of condiments with their meals, hence the amounts here. It is a good way to use green tomatoes just when the apples come in. I make this every other year, give a few jars away, and we have enough.

1. Very finely mince fruits and vegetables. Drain.

2. Mix all ingredients and simmer until tender. Process in water bath 10 minutes in pint jars. Opened jars can be refregerated for up to a month.

1 gallon quartered green
  tomatoes
1 gallon quartered apples
4 bell peppers
1 bunch celery
1 quart vinegar
2 cups honey
1 teaspoon cloves
1 teaspoon allspice
1 teaspoon salt
1 teaspoon mustard seeds

D.V.'s Mincemeat

12 medium sized green
   tomatoes
4 cups honey
2 cups raisins
5 medium cooking apples,
   peeled and minced
1 Tablespoon salt
1 Tablespoon cinnamon
1 Tablespoon allspice
1 Tablespoon cloves

1. **Mince tomatoes and drain.**

2. **Simmer tomatoes until tender with 1 cup honey.**

3. **Combine all the ingredients and simmer 45 minutes.**

4. **Process in water bath 10 minutes in pint jars.
Opened jars can be refrigerated one to two weeks.**

Eggplant Aside

1. **Peel and lightly steam eggplant.**

2. **Heat oil and sesame seeds in a skillet. Add the vegetables except the tomato and saute lightly.**

3. **Add tomatoes, honey, vinegar, and spices. Simmer on low heat about 20 minutes. Keeps in refrigerator two weeks.**

1 eggplant
4 tomatoes, chopped
1 cup chopped cabbage
1 stalk celery, chopped
1/4 cup pickled nasturtium
    pods
1/2 cup olive oil
1/4 cup tarragon vinegar or
    other herbed vinegar
2 teaspoons honey
2 teaspoons sesame seeds
salt and pepper to taste

Herb Butters

These can be made with many different herbs or combinations of herbs. Keep experimenting. I'm growing six different kinds of basil this summer to find out which basil butter goes best on tomato sandwiches.

For each quarter pound of butter, use one teaspoon chopped fresh herb. When you get to know their flavors and uses, try a few combinations. We like one herb at a time; these are our favorites:

marjoram
dill
chive
basil
tarragon

Chop herb very fine and blend into softened butter. Let sit overnight to absorb flavors best.

Lemon Honey Jelly

This is good with spicy or fried foods. I also give the kids a teaspoonful if they are coughing at night.

1. **Boil the honey and water.**

2. **Add pectin and boil 2 minutes more.**

3. **Remove from heat and stir in lemon juice.**

4. **Pour into 1/2 pint jars and seal.**

1/3 cup fresh lemon juice
6 ounces liquid pectin
5 cups honey
1 1/2 cups water

Nut Cream

Tastes nice on puddings, fruit gels, or on cold baked apples.

Whiz all ingredients in a blender.

*1 cup raw cashews or
   almonds
1/4 cup honey
2 cups water
dash of vanilla
pinch salt*

Nut Milk

Cream all ingredients in a blender. Add salt and honey to taste.

*1 cup raw nuts
1 quart boiling water*

Nut Milk Mayonnaise

This can be used in recipes calling for mayonnaise or Tofu Mayonnaise.

1. Process all but oil and lemon juice in a blender.

2. With blender still going, drizzle in the oil.

3. When thick, stir in the lemon juice or vinegar. Keeps in refrigerator up to two weeks.

1 cup thick nut milk
1 1/2 cups oil
1/4 cup lemon juice or
*   vinegar*
3 Tablespoons honey
1/2 teaspoon salt or to taste
1/2 teaspoon dillseed
1/2 teaspoon paprika
1 Tablespoon prepared
*   mustard*

Peach Chutney

5 peaches, peeled and
  chopped
6 ripe tomatoes, peeled and
  chopped
5 green apples, chopped
1 green pepper, chopped
3/4 cup honey
1/2 cup vinegar
1 teaspoon ginger powder
1 teaspoon mustard seeds
1 teaspoon salt

1. Simmer all but honey for about 20 minutes.

2. Stir in honey and simmer until thick.

3. Process in water bath 10 minutes in pint jars.

Pesto Sentio

1. **Bring water to a boil and add hing.**

2. **Boil 2 minutes and process in blender with cashews.**

3. **Add basil and puree until smooth. Season to taste.**

2 cups fresh basil
1 cup cashews
2 pinches hing
1/2 cup water
salt to taste

Picada

This recipe is a nice thing to do with a bumper crop of hazel-nuts. Try it wrapped in a pita pocket or a Yeasty Crepe (p. 29); do this on site or it will be soggy.

1 cup tofu, cubed
1 cup tomatoes, chopped
1 cup eggplant, chopped
1 green pepper, chopped
1/2 cup black olives, chopped
    and set aside

Paste:
1/4 teaspoon hing
1/4 teaspoon saffron
1/4 teaspoon salt
1/4 teaspoon cinnamon
1 teaspoon fresh chopped
    parsley
1/2 cup toasted almonds
1/2 cup toasted hazelnuts
1/2 cup water

1. Chop tofu, tomatoes, eggplant and pepper and set aside.

2. Make paste by grinding ingredients in a blender or food processor.

3. Add paste to vegetables.

4. Simmer until tender.

5. When cool add 1/2 cup chopped black olives.

Quick Ketchup

1. **Simmer all together for about 20 minutes or until thick.**

2. **Remove bay leaf and puree in a blender.**

2 quarts tomato puree

6 ounces tomato paste

2 teaspoons salt

3 green peppers, chopped

1 Tablespoon celery seed

1 1/2 teaspoons allspice

1 1/2 teaspoons cloves

1/2 bay leaf

3/4 cup honey

1/4 cup molasses

1 1/2 cups cider vinegar

Rhubarb Sauce

This makes a good dipping sauce for Falafels (p. 105), Pakora (p. 115), or Garbanzo Chips (p. 18).

1 1/2 cups stewed rhubarb
1/2 cup honey
1 teaspoon dijon mustard
juice of 1/2 lemon
1/4 teaspoon salt
pinch wasabi powder

Combine all ingredients.

Spanish Hazelnut Sauce

Puree all ingredients together and simmer for 20 minutes.

2 Tablespoons chopped fresh
   basil
1/4 teaspoon hing
1/2 cup toasted hazelnuts
1/2 cup toasted almonds
1 cup tomato puree
1/2 cup olive oil
1 Tablespoon cider vinegar
1 Tablespoon molasses

Soy Cream

1. **Whiz milk in a blender on high speed, dribbling oil in slowly.**

2. **Add remaining ingredients and chill. Use it like Nut Cream (p. 150) on puddings, fruit gels, pie, etc.**

1/2 cup soy milk
1 cup oil
3 Tablespoons honey
1 teaspoon vanilla
pinch salt

Sunflower Seed Sauce

Process all ingredients in blender, salt to taste.

1 cup sunflower seeds
1/3 cup water
2 Tablespoons lemon juice

Sweet and Sour Sauce

Traditional with Spring Rolls (p. 130) but good with any fried food. Try it with Tempura (p. 133), Corn Fritters (p. 101) or Falafels (p. 105).

1. **Simmer fruits in water until tender.**

2. **Mash gently and stir in remaining ingredients. Simmer 5 minutes more. Keeps in refrigerator up to two weeks.**

6 cups chopped fruit
   (peaches, plums,
   pineapples)
1 1/2 cups water
1 Tablespoon tamari
1/2 cup honey
1/2 teaspoon salt
1 Tablespoon arrowroot or
   cornstarch or tapioca flour
1/3 cup cider vinegar

Tofu Mayonnaise

1 1/2 pounds tofu
2 Tablespoons tahini
1 teaspoon dill seed
1/4 cup vinegar
2 Tablespoons prepared
   mustard
1/2 teaspoon turmeric
   (optional)
1/4 cup honey
1/3 cup oil
salt to taste

The oil can be left out of this recipe to make it low in fat. It has plenty of protein on a whole grain bread, so I often make sandwiches simply of sliced vegetables and Tofu Mayonnaise.

Whiz all ingredients in blender. Add milk if needed to desired consistency. Adjust the seasonings to suit your taste.

Variation:
For spicy Tofu Mayonnaise: add 1/8 cup wasabi powder, 1 drop chili oil, and a few drops tamari to each 1/4 cup Tofu Mayonnaise.

Tofu Tartar Sauce

1 cup Tofu Mayonnaise
1 cup D.V.'s Relish (p. 145)
1 Tablespoon pickled
   nasturtium pods or capers
   (optional)

Stir all together. Keeps in the refrigerator for 2 weeks.

SNACKS

Crunchings and Munchings

This mix was named for a beloved book friend, Gurgi. It is gorp (the stuff you eat on hiking trips), lightened up with puffed cereal. Mix in proportions suitable to your taste.

1/2 cup raisins

1/2 cup chopped dried apples

1/2 cup sunflower seeds

1/2 cup almonds

1/2 cup chocolate or carob chips

1 cup puffed rice

Momo Chips

Momo is a little Tibetan girl who sustains herself on a long journey through the mountains sucking on beads made of yak cheese. These are made of soy milk, not yak milk, but romantic mothers tend to have romantic kids; mine named these.

Dried yuba sheets can be purchased at an oriental market or they can be made at home by lifting off the skin formed on a simmered pan of soy milk. The skin is dried and called yuba. These are very rich in protein.

Break yuba into bite-sized pieces or deep fry the sheets until golden brown and break into bite sized chips. Drain and lightly salt.

Party Mix

6 Tablespoons margarine
1/4 teaspoon salt
1/2 teaspoon chili powder
   (or curry powder)
1 Tablespoon tamari
3 cups Corn Chex cereal
3 cups Wheat Chex cereal
3/4 cup roasted nuts

1. Melt the margarine in a flat shallow baking dish.

2. Add the Chex and nuts and spices. Stir well.

3. Spread out single layer thick and bake 20 minutes at 250°.
Cool to crisp. Store in airtight container for several weeks.

Variation:
Use mini Shredded Wheat instead of Chex.

Popcorn

Popcorn can be flavored to make different snacks. Try one of
the following:

   parmesan cheese
   chili powder
   curry powder
   nutritional yeast (my kids' favorite)

Soy Curds

This can be used as a non-dairy replacement for cottage cheese. It doesn't taste the same, but has the same consistency. When someone in the family can't eat dairy products, this sometimes goes in a lunch with sweetened stewed fruit or pineapple chunks.

1. Mix flour and water. Stirring over low heat, simmer 15 minutes.

2. Remove from heat and fold in the lemon juice or vinegar and salt.

3. Let it cool for about 1/2 hour. Drain in cheese cloth for a few hours.

1/2 cup soy flour
1 pint water
1/2 teaspoon salt
2 Tablespoon vinegar or
  lemon juice

Soynuts or Chickpea Nuts

1. **Wash soybeans.**

3 cups water

1 cup dry soybeans or
*   chickpeas*

oil

2. **Soak soybeans in water for 2 days, changing water when necessary.**

3. **Drain and dry the water from the soybeans.**

4. **Fry in preheated hot oil until golden. Drain on paper towels and salt lightly. When cool, store in airtight containers. Stores up to two weeks.**

Variation:
Soak soybeans in salted water overnight. Roast on unoiled baking sheet, one layer deep, in 250° oven for about two hours, stirring occasionally.

Variation:
Use chickpeas instead of soybeans and add salt to the water on the second day of soaking instead of salting later.

Spiced Nuts

1. **Mix nuts and oil in a baking dish, and bake 20 - 30 minutes at about 300°. Stir occasionally.**

2. **Remove from oven and stir in mixed spices. Cool to crisp. Store in airtight container.**

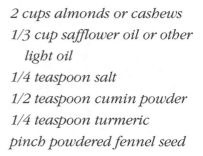

2 cups almonds or cashews

1/3 cup safflower oil or other light oil

1/4 teaspoon salt

1/2 teaspoon cumin powder

1/4 teaspoon turmeric

pinch powdered fennel seed

Toasting Nuts and Seeds

Nuts and seeds can be toasted on a dry cast-iron skillet, stirring often, or roasted in the oven, at about 300°, stirring less often. Cool before storing airtight so that they will remain crunchy.

Vegetable and Fruit Ideas

Vegetable Slices:

Fresh vegetables are wonderful for scooping up dips. Try slicing them in different shapes to better enjoy their wonderful textures and flavors:

matchsticks
long flats
ovals made by slicing a cone or cylinder, such as carrots,
    zucchini or cucumbers, at an angle

A handful of snap beans or snap peas are already perfectly prepared. Turnip or rutabaga or kohlrabi are delicious sliced thin as chips. If you are preparing broccoli for supper, save the stalks to cut into long flats for lunch the following day. My children like to eat frozen peas or corn like peanuts. I thought them weird, but corn and peas turn out to be highly desired trading items at school lunch times.

Dried Vegetables and Fruit:

Slice carrots, zucchini, or bananas thinly and place on a mesh tray in a dehydrator until crunchy, or use a cookie sheet in a very low temperature oven. Turn over when one side is crisp. Use the vegetable "chips" with dip in place of potato chips. Cut corn can also be dehydrated and turns out nice and crunchy.

Dehydrating Fruits and Leathers:

These are incredibly easy to make, especially with a dehydrator. They keep for months and nicely use up the glut of
fruit we get at some seasons.

To make leather, remove pit or seeds from fruit. Put fruit in a
blender with enough water to blend. Pour the resulting puree
on a plastic drying sheet and dehydrate on low until leathery.

If using a parked car back window, oven, or other heat
source, pour the puree on waxed paper on a tray or cookie
sheet, expose to gentle heat and leave room for air circulation
(crack open oven door or car window).

Leathers can be eaten plain or filled. Roll a piece around a
cheese finger or spread with cream cheese and roll up.
(Sliced, these become Fruit and Cream Pinwheels.)

Jam:

Jam can be made by dehydrating puree 1/2 way to leather. It
can be sweetened if desired. We make a brilliant scarlet
strawberry jam this way.

Yogurt Chips:

These can be made by dropping little bits of flavored yogurt
on a plastic tray and dehydrating.

Chapter 7

Desserts

Table of Contents

CHAPTER SEVEN: DESSERTS

Great lunches can be centered around a dessert. Squash pie with a green salad or cheesecake and clear vegetable soup— many recipes you would traditionally think of as dessert are high in protein and quite worthy on their own.

Tofu is a good egg substitute and soy flour can replace some of the wheat flour in a recipe, to boost the protein. Sneak in nuts and seeds (they can be powdered and go undetected). Cream cheese, ricotta cheese, and pureed cottage cheese can be added to almost anything; apple pie tastes great with cheese in it or in the crust: "apple pie without some cheese is like a kiss without a squeeze!"

Vegetables are also easy to get into desserts. Many of the milder vegetables such as beets, corn, lima beans, and pota- toes can be used in the liquid portion of a recipe. Squash, yams and carrots can be added to cakes and cookies to lend moistness and nutrition. When I bake something chocolate I always add spinach powder or puree!

Egg Replacer for Baking

To replace 2 eggs:

1/2 pound tofu

2 Tablespoons yogurt

1 Tablespoon cornstarch or
arrowroot

1/2 teaspoon baking soda

Process in blender or food processor.

Applesauce Slush

This was discovered by accident but greeted with great enthusiasm. Freeze any amount of applesauce.

The morning of lunch packing, place it in a plastic thermos or container and by noon—voila—slush! It's easiest to get out if you freeze it in a straight-sided container. If you freeze it in small yogurt cups, they can be packed into lunches straight from the freezer.

Baked Sweet Potato

Bake a sweet potato for 45 minutes in a 350° oven. Send it in its skin. Peel and eat like a banana.

Cheese Fruit Mousse

1. **Chop fruit, saving juices.**

2. **Mix 1 1/2 cups juice with arrowroot flour and simmer until quite thick (if chopping fruits doesn't yield enough juice, add apple or orange juice to make up the difference).**

3. **Remove from heat and stir in the ricotta cheese and yogurt, then add fruits and cheddar.**

4. **Chill for a few hours and grate some nutmeg on top.**

1 peach, finely diced
1 apple, finely diced
1 banana, finely diced
1/2 cup chopped pineapple
1 orange
1/2 cup quartered grapes
   or to save time, use 3 - 4
   cups of leftover fruit salad
   in place of the above
   ingredients
1/2 cup arrowroot flour
1/2 cup ricotta cheese
1/2 cup yogurt
3/4 cup grated mild cheddar
   cheese
pinch nutmeg

Cream Cheese Frosting

1 part honey
1 part butter [or margine]
1 part cream cheese

Soften cream cheese and butter, then mix all together until smooth. Rich!

Crunchy Chip Cookies

1/2 cup honey
1/2 cup oil
1 cup water
1/2 cup toasted sunseeds
1/2 cup toasted sesame seeds
1 cup cracked millet
2 cups rolled oats
1 1/2 cups whole wheat flour
1 cup chocolate or carob
   chips

1. Mix together oil, honey, and water.

2. Stir in remaining ingredients. Drop by teaspoonsful onto an oiled cookie sheet. Press to flatten into cookie shape.

3. Bake at 350° for 20 minutes.

Date Nut Bars

1. Cook dates in water until soft and thick (if they don't melt into a thick puree, puree in blender, then cook on low heat a few minutes more). Stir in lemon juice. Set aside. This is the filling.

2. Grind rolled oats to a gritty flour. Mix with flour, salt, and honey, then with melted butter. This is the crust.

3. Press half the crust into a buttered baking dish.

4. Spread on filling, then crumble the rest of the oat mixture on top (I use a cheese grater to get an even crumble). Bake at 350° for 1/2 hour. Cool then cut in squares.

2 cups dates

1 cup water

1 teaspoon lemon juice

2 cups oats or rye

1 cup flour

1/2 teaspoon salt

1 cup honey

1/4 pound butter
  [or margarine], melted

1 cup chopped walnuts
  (Sprinkled on top)

Fruit Agar Gel Mold
(a vegetarian gelatin dessert)

3 cups fruit juice
  (try grapefruit or
  tangerine)
1 Tablespoon agar
  (granulated)
2 cups chopped fruit (apples,
  oranges, bananas, grapes,
  etc.)
1/2 cup chopped nuts,
  coconut, or sunflower
  seeds

1. Chop up all the fruits and drain, saving juice.

2. Add nuts.

3. Mix agar with fruit juice in a sauce pan and allow to sit for a few minutes.

4. Bring to a boil and boil 3 minutes, stirring.

5. Remove from heat, let cool a bit, fold in fruit mix.

6. Pour into a mold and refrigerate for 1 - 2 hours, until solid. Stays solid at room temperature.

Halva

1. Stir together tahini, honey, soy milk powder, and carob powder at room temperature.

2. Press into a flat pan about 3/4 inch deep.

3. Sprinkle top with the nuts and press into mixture. Refrigerate about 2 hours. Slice.

2 cups tahini
3/4 cup honey
1 1/2 cups soy milk powder
1/2 cup carob powder
1/2 cup chopped pecans

1 1/2 cups whole wheat
    pastry flour
1 stick melted butter
    [or margarine]
1 teaspoon soda
1/2 teaspoon salt
3/4 cup honey
1 1/2 Tablespoons vinegar
1 cup water
1 cup currants

Honey Cakes

Basic Medieval Honey Cake

1. **Whisk all ingredients together and stir in currants.**

2. **Bake in an ungreased 8x8 or 9x9 pan at 350° for about 1/2 hour or until done.**

Lemon Cake

Omit currants. Add grated rind of 1 lemon, juice of one lemon, and 1 teaspoon lemon extract.

Spice Cake

Omit currants. Use molasses in place of honey and add 1 cup mashed squash or sweet potato. Reduce water to 1/2 cup and add 1/2 teaspoon each ginger, cloves, cinnamon.

Chocolate or Carob Cake

Omit currants. Add 4 Tablespoons carob powder or 4 Tablespoons cocoa powder, 1/4 cup more honey (to the cocoa) and 1 teaspoon vanilla.

Indian Pudding

This is a good way to use up a lot of souring milk. Nice with Nut Cream (p. 150) on top.

1. Scald the milk by simmering it to just under a boil.

2. Mix cornmeal, 1/2 cup milk, and tapioca and add to the scalded milk. Simmer 20 minutes, stirring.

3. Remove 1 cup of the milk and set aside.

4. Add remaining ingredients.

5. Pour all into a buttered baking dish.

6. Pour remaining 1 cup milk over the top. Bake for 3 hours in slow oven. Cool to set.

4 cups scalded milk

1/2 cup milk

3/4 cup cornmeal

3 Tablespoons tapioca

1 1/2 teaspoons salt

1/2 cup honey

1 cup molasses

1 teaspoon ginger

1/2 teaspoon cinnamon

1/2 cup butter [or margarine]

1/2 pound tofu
1 cup honey
1/2 cup molasses
1 Tablespoon vanilla
1 Tablespoon vinegar
1 1/4 cups peanut butter
2 1/2 cups flour
1 teaspoon baking powder
1 teaspoon baking soda
1 1/2 teaspoons salt

Kingsmont Peanut Butter Cake

1. Process tofu and wet ingredients in a blender or food processor.

2. Stir in the dry ingredients. Bake at 350° for 1/2 hour.

Pumpkin or Squash Pie

1. Mix all ingredients in a saucepan and cook on low until thickened.

2. Pour into pie crust. Bake at 425° for 15 minutes then at 350° for 20 - 30 minutes.

3 cups mashed pumpkin or squash
2 - 3 Tablespoons cornstarch (depends upon how wet pumpkin is)
1/2 teaspoon cinnamon
1/2 teaspoon ginger
1/4 teaspoon nutmeg
1/2 teaspoon salt
1/4 teaspoon cloves
2 Tablespoons butter [or margarine]
1 cup milk [or nut milk]
1/2 cup molasses
1/2 cup honey
9 inch pie crust

Soy Prisms

2 cups soy milk
1/3 cup kuzu, powdered
  (a thickening agent
  available in oriental or
  health food stores)
1/3 cup maple syrup
4 Tablespoons toasted soy
  flour

1. Mix soy milk and kuzu and heat until it begins to thicken.

2. Add remaining ingredients and simmer, stirring constantly, until quite thick.

3. Pour into a flat bottomed shallow baking dish and smooth over the top. When completely cool this can be cut into small cubes or triangles and lifted out with a spatula.

Rainbow Prisms

1 cup cubed skinned peaches
  or mangoes
1 cup cubed pineapple
  chunks
1 cup halved red grapes
1 cup cubed honeydew
  melon
2 Tablespoons lemon juice
1 Tablespoon honey

1. Mix honey and lemon together. Pour over remaining ingredients and gently stir to coat.

2. Add Soy Prisms (from above recipe). Dribble on a bit of Cashew Cream (p. 150) just before eating.

Relative Blintzes

Wrappers:

Sometimes I use spring roll skins and fry them. Other times, I wrap the filling in several layers of filo leaves, brush with butter, and bake 20 minutes at 350°.

Filling:

2 cups ricotta cheese

1/2 cup honey

1 teaspoon vanilla or reduce honey and put a layer of fruit spread on the cheese

Rice Pudding

This is good cold or warm in a thermos; tastes good with Nut Cream (p. 150) on it.

1. Cook rice in water for 20 minutes or until the water is absorbed. The rice will still be only half cooked.

2. Stir in salt, raisins, milk, cardamom, and coriander. Simmer 20 - 30 minutes.

3. Add coconut and honey. Let set for 15 minutes.

1 cup brown rice

3/4 cup water

pinch salt

1/4 cup raisins

2 cups milk

pinch powdered cardamom

1/2 teaspoon coriander powder

1/2 cup coconut

1/2 cup honey

Sesame Pudding

1/2 cup tahini

1/2 cup arrowroot or
*   cornstarch or tapioca*
*   powder*

1/2 cup honey or barley malt

4 cups water

1 teaspoon powdered ginger

2 cups mixed: walnuts,
*   coconut, and small diced*
*   dried fruit*

1. Stir together tahini, arrowroot, honey, water and ginger. Heat slowly, stirring until thick.

2. Fold in dried fruits and nuts. Chill to set.

Squash Hermits

1. Mix dry ingredients separately from wet ones.

2. Mix together and add chopped nuts and fruits.

3. Spread out 1/2 inch thick onto an oiled cookie sheet and bake at 350° for 1/2 hour or until golden. Cool and cut into squares or rectangles.

1/4 cup soy flour
1 1/2 cups whole wheat flour
1 teaspoon baking soda
1/2 teaspoon baking powder
1/2 teaspoon salt
1/2 teaspoon cinnamon
1/2 teaspoon allspice
pinch nutmeg
1 stick soft butter
    [or margarine]
1 cup baked or steamed
    winter squash puree
3/4 cup molasses
1/2 cup chopped walnuts
1/2 cup sunflower seeds
1 cup currants or chopped
    raisins

Stuffed Dates

pitted dates
cream cheese
almonds or coconut

Slit the top of a date lengthwise, fill cavity with cream cheese and roll in walnut meal or coconut. An alternate is to press a whole almond in the cavity instead of the cream cheese.

Sumitra's Cheesecake

1. **Combine graham crackers and melted butter and press into a pie pan.**

2. **Blend filling ingredients until smooth.**

3. **Pour into the crust and bake at 350° for 40 minutes or until lightly golden on the edges.**

4. **Mix topping ingredients, spread on baked cheese cake, and bake 5 minutes more.**

Crust:
12 graham crackers, crushed
1/4 pound butter
  [or margarine], melted

Filling:
1/2 pound tofu
1 pound ricotta cheese
8 ounces cream cheese
1/2 cup milk
2 Tablespoons powdered
  tapioca or cornstarch
2 teaspoons vanilla
1/2 cup honey

Topping: *(optional)*
1 cup sour cream
1/4 cup honey
1 teaspoon vanilla

Sweet Noodle Custard

1/2 pound cream cheese
1/2 pound tofu
1/3 cup sour cream
2/3 cup honey
1/4 teaspoon vanilla
2 Tablespoons milk
2 cups cooked fettucini
3 apples, sliced

1. Sprinkle the apple slices with 1/2 teaspoon cinnamon or nutmeg. Set aside.

2. Process cream cheese, tofu, sour cream, honey, vanilla, and milk in blender or food processor.

3. Fold in the cooked fettucini.

4. In a buttered casserole, layer half the noodle mixture then half the apples. Repeat, ending with apples. Bake at 350° for 45 minutes.

Sweet Potato Pudding

1. Mix all ingredients and simmer, stirring constantly, until mixture thickens.

2. Pour into containers and sprinkle with nutmeg. Nut Cream (p. 150) on top is nice.

Variation:
Use 2 cups butternut squash instead of sweet potato, replace honey with 3/4 cup molasses, and add 1/4 teaspoon ginger, 1/4 teaspoon cinnamon, and 1/4 teaspoon cloves.

3 cups milk
2 baked sweet potatoes,
*   peeled and mashed*
1/4 cup honey
1/2 cup cornstarch
pinch salt

Tunbridge Truffles

These are named after the infamous snack food used to energize work parties erecting a post and beam house in Tunbridge, Vermont. This vegetarian pemmican, along with water, can keep you going a long time.

3 cups dried fruit
(apples, apricots, dates,
prunes, raisins)
1 cup nuts
(walnuts, hazelnuts,
sunseeds, pecans)

1. Grind everything together in a blender or food processor. Add a little lemon juice or orange juice if it's too dry.

2. Roll into ping-pong sized balls and roll in coconut or nut meal. (The children think that these need a chocolate chip for a surprise middle.)

On the Vegetarian Way of Life

The following books are available mailorder from:

NUCLEUS Publications
Rt. 2, Box 49, Willow Springs, MO 65793
Phone orders: (800) 762-6595

Send for your complimentary catalog.

What's Wrong With Eating Meat?
by Vistara Parham.
PCAP Publications
$2.50 Order # W3314.

Food for Thought
by Ananda Mitra
Nucleus Publications
$7.00 Order #FT304.

Yoga Ethics
by Vimala McClure
Nucleus Publications
$7.00 Order #YE630

Shipping:

Up to $9.99 add $3.00
$10—$14.99 add $3.50
$15—$19.99 add $4.00
$20—$29.99 add $4.50
$30—$49.99 add $5.00
$50—$99.99 add $5.50
$100 or more free

Sources for Foods

For organic foods by mailorder:

Walnut Acres
Penns Creek, PA 17862
(800) 433-3998

Send for a free catalog. They have: beans (dry and canned), canned vegetables, fruits and soups, nut butters (including tahini), whole grains and flours, pasta, oils, condiments (including tamari and miso), spices, seeds and nuts, dried fruits, cheese made with vegetable rennet.

For Indian spices:

Sultan's Delight, Inc.
P.O. Box 253
Staten Island, NY 10314
(718) 720-1557

Send for a free catalog. (Middle East and Indian spices)

For Japanese foods and spices:

Katagiri
224 E. 59th St.
New York, NY 10022
(212) 755-3566

Send for a free catalog.

For oriental, Indian and macrobiotic foods and spices:

Frontier Cooperative Herbs
The Herb and Spice Collection
P.O. Box 118
Norway, IA 52318
(800) 365-4372

About the Author

Linda Haynes lives in New Hampshire with her husband and three children. She has been a vegetarian for twenty years. She took up cooking after the birth of her first child when she and her husand settled into a "division of labor."

Cooking is one of Linda's many pursuits. Linda built the house her family lives in while finishing her master's degree in education. She is also an avid gardener and a practicing artist.

INDEX

INDEX

INDEX

SOME STILL WANT THE MOON
A Woman's Introduction to Tantra Yoga
by Vimala McClure

Yoga philosophy says that the most basic human drive is toward self-realization; that none us us, ultimately, will settle for less; *Some Still Want the Moon* is about how to tap into that drive and make it work for you. The book covers breathing and relaxation, meditation and mantra, kundalini and chakras, yoga's creation theory, yoga ethics ("behavioral yoga"); how to use affirmations and visualizations; and includes a fully illustrated section on stretches, yoga postures and yogic aerobic exercise. 122 pages, illustrated throughout, 9 x 7, $9.95.

McClure is a trustworthy guide, a spiritual friend whose advice is as calm and as sensible as our own real hearts and minds. —**The Book Reader**

Food for Thought
The Vegetarian Philosophy
by Ananda Mitra

This is an excellent resource for beginning and established vegetarians. It shows where to find the nutrients that compose a balanced, healthy vegetarian diet. It covers proteins, vitamins and minerals one by one, and points out which foods are good sources of each. There are chapters on protein combining, dietary suggestions for specific ailments, and fasting. Includes extensive tables of the nutritional composition of all the basic foods. 96 pages, 5 1/2 x 8, $7.00.